WRITINGS AND REFLECTIONS

From the World of *Roderick Haig-Brown*

WRITINGS *AND* REFLECTIONS

Edited by
Valerie Haig-Brown

McClelland and Stewart

The Canadian Publishers
McClelland and Stewart Limited
25 Hollinger Road
Toronto M4B 3G2

Canadian Cataloguing in Publication Data

Haig-Brown, Roderick L., 1908-1976.
  Writings and reflections

(From the world of Roderick Haig-Brown)
ISBN 0-7710-3766-X

I. Haig-Brown, Valerie. II. Title.

PS8515.A46W74   C818'.5208   C82-094026-7
PR9199.3.H332W74

Printed and bound in Canada

For
ANN ELMORE HAIG-BROWN
his wife and my mother

Contents

Editor's Note *9*

On British Columbia
1. Coastscape *13*
2. The Passing of Steam *20*

On Other Men
3. Alan Roderick Haig-Brown *27*
4. Hardy's Dorset *37*
5. Izaak Walton: His Friends and His Rivers *48*

On Writing and Reading
6. The Writer in Isolation: A Surprised Exploration of a Given Subject *57*
7. Writer's Notebook: Influences *66*
8. How Important is Reading? *72*
9. The Way into Books *81*

On War
10. If Armageddon's On *92*
11. The Bells *103*

On Birds and Animals
12. Places des Cygnes *111*
13. Little Girls and Horses *122*
14. Ghost Cat *124*

On The Law
15. The Lay Mind in the Law *133*

On Education and the Future
16. An Outsider Looks at Education *143*
17. Choice for Canadians – Security or Freedom *157*
18. The Quality of Living *162*

On Conservation
19. Some Approaches to Conservation *172*
20. Pollution for Profit *177*
21. Crying in the Wilderness: Wildlife *186*
22. Some Thoughts of Paradise *192*
23. Our Ocean: Garbage Dump and Cesspool *202*

Coda
24. The Drama of Our Environment *211*

Acknowledgments *221*

Editor's Note

At a banquet in Toronto a few months before he died, my father was introduced as a philosopher-author/*philosophe et auteur* (it was a federal government-sponsored dinner). I watched a pleased smile flicker across his face at the designation. It was as if a lifetime of thoughtful writing was being recognized for what he had always intended it – not just descriptions of fly-fishing or speeches on conservation or articles about his country – but the carefully considered words of a man who always spoke and wrote from deep conviction and a thorough knowledge of the subject he was discussing.

This third volume of his collected writing in the series *From the World of Roderick Haig-Brown* falls largely into two categories: autobiographical pieces on how and why he came to live and write on the Pacific Coast, about the people who influenced him, how he felt about books and writing; and essays and speeches concerning where our lives are or should be directed and why. Many of the latter he had already gathered together as a possible book under the title "Thoughts for the Times." While he was always most emphatically a writer, this particular collection reflects all of his other concerns as well. He was a father, a magistrate (later a judge), a leading conservationist, a university chancellor, a soldier, a fly-fisherman, and a thinking man who was able to express in writing so much of what he considered important.

An English teacher would likely classify all of the pieces here as essays, but the spectrum they cover, both in tone and subject matter, is so broad as to escape the dry, dull connotation of that definition. There is warmth and humour in "Little Girls and Horses," soul-searching concern in "If Armageddon's On," and angry despair in some of the later conservation pieces. The thoughtful jurist speaks out in "The Lay Mind in the Law," and the careful observer of nature

9

shares his pleasures in "Place des Cygnes." Most of all, the writer tells much of himself, sometimes as his main purpose, as in "The Writer in Isolation"; but often as anecdotal background, as in "Hardy's Dorset" or "The Bells" or "The Drama of Our Environment." As a writer, my father strove for simplicity and clarity and has often been praised for achieving exactly that. Whether he wrote of his youngest daughter as the fond father or of the future of our society as the philosopher-author, he wrote with a grace and flow that makes his intentions utterly clear.

I am often asked if, in the course of going through his papers to prepare this series, I have found out anything I didn't know about my father. The answer is no and yes. No because, much as the questioners would like a spicy story that had never been revealed before, my father delighted in telling such tales as how he got thrown out of school in England, and was never one to keep a good story of any sort to himself. And yes, because I have come to an infinitely greater understanding of both my father and myself. When you live with someone every day, that person doesn't necessarily seem remarkable – the parental advice or after-dinner anecdote seem part of daily life. It was only later, as I grew older and no longer had daily contact, that I came to realize what an extraordinary person my father was. Over the past few weeks of concentration on the material from which I have selected the pieces in this book, I have also realized how very closely my own basic philosophy of life resembles his. I thought I'd gone to so much trouble to leave home and grow up and be independent and think for myself. Well, I may have arrived at some of the same conclusions as my father did on my own, but I suspect that most of them are straight out of my environment as a child, if not acquired as part of my genetic inheritance. Fortunately for me I have no objection to such an inheritance and I hope my father's thoughts will continue to affect my own and other people's lives for many years to come.

Valerie Haig-Brown
Vancouver, 1981

1
Coastscape
(1973)

All people are regionalists, even in this day of swift though seldom easy travel. Even an island as small as Britain has its northerners, southerners, and midlanders, to say nothing of Welsh, Highland Scot and Lowland Scot, Londoner, Mancunian, Glaswegian. France has Bretons and Basques, Parisians, Alsatians, and all the others. Hereditary groupings, inbred through countless generations? I think not. I know sophisticated New Yorkers who travel frequently to Europe but even today consider the great plains an infinite wilderness and the Rocky Mountains insurmountable. I know eastern Canadians who think the country stops at the head of the lakes, and westerners who would rather never go east. I am not sure, though, that this makes either party less Canadian.

My own first experience of Canada was a summer afternoon in Vancouver, followed by an overnight steamship journey through the Inside Passage to a logging camp well beyond the reach of roads or public railroads. Since I had come from the State of Washington, the Pacific Coast woods were not new to me; there was less Douglas fir, more hemlock and true fir, much more salal, no vine maple. My companions were preponderantly Finnish, Swedish, Norwegian, Italian, even as they had been in Washington, but with this difference: most were first generation immigrants, even as I was, and many of the engineers and donkey punchers in those days of steam were Scottish or English.

In spite of the general similarities, the country seemed to me wilder, fresher, more remote and more exciting. It was river and forest and mountain on the grand scale, full of secret possibilities – hidden lakes and swamps, narrow valleys with steep-walled canyons, abundant wildlife except in the deep forest, immense salmon runs, trout in every lake and stream. But what was known about it all seemed little more than rumours and old wives' tales.

I had my preconceptions of Canada and Canadians. It is difficult to remember now precisely what they were, compounded of childhood impressions in England during World War One, the writings of Charles Roberts and Ernest Thompson Seton, the talk of one's elders and occasional accounts of school friends who were Canadian or had Canadian connections. A Canadian was a tall, lean man, quiet-spoken, keen-eyed, totally dependable in any crisis or tough undertaking. He was hardy and adaptable, having acquired many of the characteristics of the woods Indians, the plains Indians and the Arctic explorers. Canada was a land of forests and wheatfields and tundra. Canadian woods were the woods of Northern Ontario; Canadian loggers were river drivers; Canadian fishermen were dorymen on the Grand Banks. Canadian woodsmen were the best in the world.

These ideas called for some revision, though not quite along the lines one might have expected. All Canadians were not tall, nor were they calm and laconic; many were small and voluble, most were hard, driving workers through the day and loved to talk in the bunkhouses at night; to be catty – quick and sure on one's feet – was a virtue far beyond mere strength. To use brains and ingenuity in the moving of bulk and weight – huge logs, whole trees, donkey engines on sleds, crippled locomotives – was the supreme virtue. Few of my companions were woodsmen, though those few were highly

14

skilled. Most considered anything beyond the edge of the logging slash dangerous and mysterious territory; neither bird nor mammal interested them much; few were hunters, even fewer fishermen. But they were kindly and tolerant beyond most men I had known, quickly making a place for the stranger and his peculiarities, always sure and compassionate friends in time of need.

We worked long hours and long weeks, so my Canada took time to expand, but it did so. There was the talk of other Canadians, city newspapers in the mail, three or four days old, occasional copies of *Maclean's* and the *Family Herald* and *Star Weekly* which gave a firm body to the country, earthy and inland. Ottawa was dim at a distance, Toronto was stolid and remote, Montreal gleaming and equally remote. But Maritimers we knew at first hand, because a few of them worked with us, and there were loggers who still went back to harvest prairie wheat.

Gradually I came to know commercial fishermen, trappers, game wardens, coal miners, and stump ranchers, and the Canadian image of calm self-dependence renewed itself. The rivers became familiar places and the Pacific Coast forest was more Canadian than the Ontario woods; the bounty of the sea came to salmon purse seiners, gill-netters and trollers and to the splendid white halibut long-liners that passed northward with their nested dories. Even Vancouver, with Woodward's welcoming beacon flashing over the harbour and the bright lights of Granville and Hastings promising urban adventure, had become familiar. All together, it was less than Canada, no doubt; but it was the Canada I knew, and I loved it.

A year of exile in London, not altogether of my own choosing, taught me homesickness. It was by no means a dull time, as I scratched for an uncertain living with newspapers and magazines, scrambled through love affairs, published my first book, and wrote a good part of the second one. But the rivers were tame and tiny, there were no mountains, not even a rock bluff; there were no mauve and purple twilights with trolling lines cutting the tide-rippled water. The people were set in their ways and their places, unchanging, and I, though native-born, was a stranger.

I think I knew then that I was Canadian, that I might go elsewhere but my heart would settle for nowhere else. There was nothing I wanted to write of except Canada, the part of Canada I knew, and nothing that I wanted to know so much more of. I could not bear not to be a part of it. Most of all, I wanted to be with people who knew what I was talking about and to feel at one with all those I met and dealt with – something I had experienced in Canada and nowhere else.

Exile's dreams, perhaps, to some extent now recollected in tranquillity. But I have checked them against my cursive diary of the time and found that all the elation was fully realized. I returned instantly to my own concerns, fresh water and salt, canoes and gasboats, woods and wildlife, logs and hand tools. Within a month I had twice almost drowned myself and life was real again, instead of London.

In one sense it was a different Canada I had returned to. The Depression had started, jobs were hard to get, and paid only enough to cover board and work clothes. So we made our own jobs, jacking logs off the beaches, setting out traps (fur prices held up well), trolling for salmon, even guiding occasional fishermen and hunters. Upcoast people were fortunate; the Depression hit hard, but the bounty of the land was still with them and they were in large degree equipped to live off the land.

Canada expanded again for me when I moved south to central Vancouver Island and found myself among children of the first settlers, even some of the first settlers themselves. This is living history and should be a part of the consciousness of every Canadian. One felt a share in it, because the business of the first settlers was, and still is, unfinished business. There still is a country to be moulded, guided, shaped, brought nearer to the heart's desire. And through the early settlers the way into the country's still earlier history, the time of explorers, travellers, testers, and searchers, was opened and brought to life.

A single man is footloose and uncommitted. Marriage is a form of commitment, the birth of children a still firmer one. My wife, Ann, was American born, American raised and educated, of a Canadian mother. Her adoption of Canada progressed at least as rapidly as my own, and we knew from the start that we wanted our children to be Canadians. At that time, marriages between Canadians and Americans were probably more usual than they are today, especially in the Maritimes and the Pacific Northwest. The border was of minor importance and nearly everyone had close relatives and relationships on both sides. Identity was not lessened by this; it was in itself a special identity, another aspect of Canadianism. If we have grown away from it, I believe it is loss rather than gain.

Perhaps a Canadian's Canada should not be a continuously expanding idea; surely at some stage one accepts, adopts, believes firmly and forever. In a sense this may be so. But even physically, apart from its splendid diversity of people, Canada is a huge country, and for many of us, native-born as well as immigrants, World War Two was our first full appreciation of this immensity and diversity. We were whisked from one end of the country to the other at the whim of remote authorities. We were mixed and mingled and understood each other – units from the Coast, the Maritimes, Ontario, Quebec, and the Prairies brigaded together, full brothers, Canadians, no longer provincials. It was a proud feeling, not simply because we wore the country's uniform but because we understood each other, trusted each other, and felt we were together. We were mixed and shuffled and changed in training camps and transit camps and reinforcement units, proclaiming our provincial loyalties at every stage but knowing full well how little they meant in the larger loyalty.

My own experience was enriched and deepened by several

months' service on loan to the RCMP. In the course of this I spent time in every province, in the Yukon and the Northwest Territories. I was aboard the St. Roch shortly before she sailed for the Northwest Passage, visited the Caughnawaga Indian people in the south and the Read Island Eskimos in the north, caught Atlantic salmon in Nova Scotia, and Arctic grayling by Bloody Falls on the Coppermine. I studied the workings of prairie detachments and the people they served, learned the charm of Fredericton, watched the Bay of Fundy tides, understood that the ways of the Maritimes are not always the ways of British Columbia, even though both are Canadian. Through the RCMP, its background and performance, I learned one more side of the history of Canada and glimpsed something of the sources of power in Ottawa.

This, then, became my Canada at firsthand. I have reinforced it and filled in further details in the past twenty-five years and no doubt shall continue to do so.

Canada has left me free to make a life and has provided most of the material for that life. There have been dissensions and disappointments in it and strivings that achieved little or nothing, but these belong in every life. I have been challenged constantly to learn and try to understand a new, unwritten land, and I have shared that land with many people also trying to find their way in it, trying to shape it into meaning for themselves and for others. It was a great endeavour; it still goes on and it will go on.

In Canada my children are free to make their lives as they would be nowhere else – less free perhaps than I was, because there are now more people; more free because there are now more ways. They will not become wealthy and I would not wish that for them any more than I have wished it for myself. But they have learned, in the public schools and public universities of the country, how to serve. They have found opportunities for service and they will constantly make or find others. If the world in which they serve is not a secure one, I question that this is new, though the degree of insecurity may be. In Canada, they are as well placed as anywhere to work for greater security for themselves and for all mankind.

I love the yield of the Canadian land and water, forest and grain and grass and cattle, fish, and wild creatures. It is on this and from this that the people of Canada, directly or indirectly, have their being. It is in searching out the land, learning to live in it, learning to use it, that we have been shaped and tempered. We have made many mistakes, some wilful, some founded in ignorance, and we have not always shaped ourselves well. But I love the best of our intentions, hopes and desires, and I love the soul of Canada, the striving for unity and justice that exists in some degree in all of us. I believe in the essential quality of the people of Canada, as I believe in myself and my children; and I wish us all a land fit to live in so long as we are prepared to keep it and build it that way for the sake of others as well as ourselves.

If this sounds like a hymn of love to the land that has made our lives and the people we have lived among, it is exactly that, from my wife Ann and myself – two immigrants of forty or fifty years ago who expected much, found much, and know there is still much more to find.

2

The Passing of Steam
(1953)

Nearly twenty-eight years ago, I hired out for the first time in a Pacific Coast logging camp. I had little idea what to expect of it. I supposed one rode down a river on logs that eventually disappeared into a sawmill; my chief worry was about getting off the logs before they started through the saws, but I assumed that someone had already worked this out, since loggers were not yet in short supply.

I needn't have worried. The water that moved the big Pacific Coast logs was steam, not flood. For the next six or seven years my world was railroads and trestle bridges, steam donkeys, steel cables, gigantic blocks, speeders, switches, rock-cuts, curves, tangents, run-arounds, tail-tracks, switchbacks; and always the locomotives, One-spot or Five-spot, Ten-spot or Two-spot, Shays, Climaxes, straight-connected Baldwins. And the men I worked with were men who had utter faith in steam as the most flexible, powerful, and beautiful mover of mass weight in the history of invention.

It seemed to us then that the technique of logging had reached its peak, that nothing could be faster or more efficient or more brutally powerful than the steam monsters we served—skidders that swung three and four great logs at a turn across canyons and valleys, bringing them twelve hundred, fifteen hundred, even two or three thousand feet from the bush to the tracks; high-lead machines that roared throaty answer to the signal whistle, tightening their heavy sky lines, rattling the chokers, cracking the logs free from tangled ground six or eight hundred feet from the spar-tree; and the locomotives, seventy-ton geared Shays that dragged empty cars up four-per-cent grades and clattered back down with the loads from the logging sides; the hundred-and-twenty-ton straight-connected Baldwins on the mainline, swinging grandly down to the beach twice a day with sixty or more loads of logs behind them.

In a sense we were right. We were moving the stuff as it never had been moved before and never will be again, tearing away the great Douglas fir stands of Oregon, Washington, and British Columbia from flat and valley and sidehill. As the timber grew smaller, the stands farther back in the mountains, so diesel motors and gas motors and rubber tires and Caterpillar tractors grew better and more efficient. And the thing we had believed could never happen began to happen; trucks began to take over from locomotives and skeleton cars, Caterpillars began to replace skidders and high-lead machines; the fast, hard-hitting power of explosion-driven pistons matched the new conditions better than the smooth, flexible infinity of steam.

Today the replacement is almost complete. Twenty years ago a "truck-show" was something small, probably haywire; the wise logger avoided it unless he knew it. Today, every show, large or small, is a truck show. On Vancouver Island, only one bit of railroad operation is left, on the Nimpkish watershed in the far north. One by one the others have folded or converted; Campbell River Timber, Salmon River Logging, Merrill and Ring, Comox Logging and Railway, the MacMillan operations, Bloedel operations, Malahat Logging, Thompson Clarke, and the others. The most recent conversion, still not complete, is the Elk River Timber Company, I.T., or the old International Timber Company to loggers who

21

remember the benevolent tyranny of little Pete Haramboure, the Basque who was one of the great steam logging superintendents.

It is a sad thing to see, is the passing of steam, for the old machines were mighty things and lovely in their way; and they go, not to other uses, but to scrap. Krupp steel, steel of the original CPR mainline, steel used in a dozen other places before it bent under the Douglas fir loads, will lose its shape and history in the furnaces; the unit from Side One, the skidder from Side Two, the balky, under-powered rigging goat, will never turn a drum under steam again – loaded on cars that will be wrecked for their wheels and bunks and air cylinders and couplings, they roll to the scrap barges at the beach; here are the great mainline and haulback blocks and the skidder bicycles, marvels of smoothness and strength, inert on the condemned flatcars; mulligan wagons with their sides pushed in, cabooses with cockeyed stovepipes and broken windows, speeders, tank cars, wood cars, coal cars, all are scrap, wood for burning, metal for the furnaces; even the locomotives, precise and intricate patterns of steel and brass and bronze, most vibrant and imposing and mysterious of all machines, still busy with the shunting and shuffling of all this junk to destruction, are themselves tomorrow's junk. They will deadhead down at last, cut to the end of the tail-track to be loaded, fires drawn, boilers dry, valves silent, on the barges and towed to town by diesel tugs.

Yet it is the men of steam rather than the machines that are clearest in the mind. The mainline locomotive at Englewood was the Five-spot, probably the biggest Shay I ever saw. She was clean and shiny and beautiful, and her passing made the ground tremble underfoot; but rather than the locomotive herself, I remember the quiet, competent bulk of Dad Hinton in the cab, his face and eyes absorbed in the massive movement under him, his body relaxed, one gauntleted hand on the air brake, an arm on the sill of the cab, in the pose of locie engineers since Watt first watched his kettle.

Dad's two sons, Charlie and Seymour, were his brakemen, and they added up to a smart mainline crew under the old man's stern control. But Dad could smile down at you from his cab with exalted benevolence; if you were a young surveyor, hitching a ride from one camp to another, he could even wait for you, with sixty loads hooked up ready to go and all those tons of hissing steel quivering under his hand.

I think, too, of Blondy Johnson, the tiny skidderman whose fireman kept a pot of coffee everlastingly on the boil in his firebox. Blondy spoke in a faint whisper and drank coffee from dawn till dusk because his lungs had been burned by gas in the first war and he was in constant pain. But his hands on the levers were so sure and gentle that he never broke his slack-line or other rigging, as most skiddermen did, and he could lay the heaviest turn of logs so softly on the landing that nothing else moved. Blondy was quick and watchful as he was gentle; and his landings were the safest I ever worked.

I remember Louie Petersen, the foreman at Camp 9, as he would sit in the office at the end of the day, head cocked to listen to the rumble of the loads passing through camp, saying softly to himself, over and over: "Lawgs, lawgs, lawgs."

And Joe Piccolo, Italian handyman in the same camp, red-faced, and always with a red handkerchief knotted at his throat; there seemed to be nothing Joe could not do, from running a speeder to running locomotive, from handling the loading levers to rigging a tree or starting a pump. And Bill Hope the timekeeper, ex-sergeant major of the RCMP, who loved the great machines so well that he kept every known spare part ready in the camp warehouse and knew where each one fitted.

Railroading in the sidehill country where the timber grew was never easy. We ran one line out to where we faced a choice between bridging three swamps, each over a thousand feet across, or turning into a sidehill that was a mile or more of solid rock. One mainline had twenty-four trestle bridges in seven miles, and rock-cut between them all. Four-per-cent grades were common, even six-per-cent was not unusual on the spur-lines. Yet railroad accidents were few. Cars jumped the tracks sometimes, as is bound to happen. Occasionally a string of loads broke loose from the snubbing line and went over the de-rail in a chaos of spilled logs and broken cars; once a speeder-load of big shots, inspecting the operation, was ditched by a de-rail someone had forgotten to lift, and since no one was seriously hurt the whole camp was made happy. Occasionally a speeder met a train on the same track, to the detriment of the speeder; my good friend Ted Thompson was killed in this way, but Ted had started from camp, as he often had before, expecting to reach the switch to Side One before the train came down from Side Two. Once, at least to my knowledge, two locomotives came face to face through the morning mist and ground to a stop only yards apart because their engineers were quick men. Billy Gordon, who had run mainline trains for the CPR, was one of the engineers, and few men can have loved or understood loco-motives more thoroughly than Billy.

Very rarely a trestle bridge would break under the load of a train, with tragic effect. It happened once at a camp I worked in down in Washington – a hot slash fire had run under a sixty-foot trestle the summer before, cooking the piles to brittleness, and the bridge broke under the weight of a locomotive the following spring, killing the engineer and the fireman. Alvin Parkin, a neighbour of mine, remembers the stormy night when he came towards a high trestle over Greenstone Creek, caught the reflection of his headlight on water that should not have been there, and dynamited his train to a standstill much too close to the flood-ripped gap where he had crossed the bridge an hour before.

But I think runaway was the most lively fear of the train crews. It takes plenty of braking power to bring a seventy-ton locomotive and five or six hundred tons of logs safely down curving, four-per-cent grades. Any failure is a terrifying and probably fatal experience. I have seen only one full-fledged runaway, but I had a ringside seat for that. The Three-spot at Camp 8, a seventy-ton Shay, had a slow and cautious engineer and a brand-new head brakeman, who was expected to speed things up. I came over the hill back into camp shortly before noon of his first morning on the job, stopped at the cookhouse for a cup of coffee and went on over to the office. Then I heard the Three-spot coming, fast, very much faster than lanky old Evans would push her, I knew, and considerably faster than any loaded train should hit a heavy downgrade. She bucketed round the curve above camp, stayed with the tracks somehow, then swept magnificently down the long, straight stretch, sheets of fire blazing from the engine brakes, the loads rocking behind her, spilling not a single log. She went through camp like a ghost train, heedless and fast, no one in the cab, no one on the loads, on past the filing shack, past the cookhouse and the car shop, with all the switches set right. On the level tail-track past the dump she slowed a little and a crew aboard might have saved her. But the end was inevitable. She ran out of track, plunged over on her side and plowed a way down to the edge of the lake. Something touched off her whistle and she set up a wail that lasted as a dozen loads of logs piled after her, one by one, slowly and relentlessly building a mountain of shattered debris that took a full month to straighten out.

Fifteen minutes later, first-aid kit in hand, I met the train crew walking down the track. It was a relief to see that they could walk, but I suspected they had jumped pretty early in the affair.

"She stay on?" Evans asked me.

"Right to the end," I said. "Used up all the track there was."

"You don't have to tie a can on us. We'll be going down in the morning."

We had to sort the story out for ourselves, though it wasn't hard to do. The new brakeman hadn't bothered to couple the air brakes through to the last twenty cars.

25

I wonder what old Evans (that wasn't his name, of course) thinks of the passing of steam, and what his young English fireman thinks. I wonder about some of the other old steam loggers – Carl Catlssen, Louis Peterson, Oscar Rose, who fell under a skeleton car and walked into camp to get first aid for the stump of the arm he had left on the track, Rough-house Pete, who raised the Three-spot from the lake, Dunc Thew, Red Fitzgerald, Black Andy, and a dozen others. I wonder about the blacksmiths and machinists and car knockers, the dispatchers and firemen and brakemen and speeder men. There are other jobs, of course, and men fit into them. But what is an engineer without his Johnson bar and his air brakes, without the sacred sill of his sacred cab, his worn cushion, his battered, infallible pocket-watch? What does Dad Hinton think or Morton Ford or Tommy Pearkes or Billy Gordon?

I could ask some of them, I suppose, and find out. There's Andy Teck who brought the Five-spot into the Elk River Camp on her first trip in 1927, a straight-connected Porter brand, spanking new, and shining in every visit. He'll deadhead her down on her last trip in a few days now, shut off the steam and set the brakes for the last time. I could ask Andy Teck what he thinks. But I doubt if I will. It seems to me I know.

3
Alan Roderick Haig-Brown
(1951)

My father was killed by machine-gun fire at Bapaume in France on March 25, 1918, while commanding an outflanked battalion in a rearguard action. I was ten years old at the time, and had seen very little of him during the previous four years, so I could not have known him well, in the ordinary sense of the word. Yet today, thirty-three years later, I remember him as clearly and vividly as I remember anyone I have met since. And, because he was a writer as well as a schoolteacher and a soldier, I know a good deal about how he thought and what he was.

Alan Roderick Haig-Brown was an Edwardian; one of the young, the strong, the brave and the fair, who had faith in their nation, their world, and themselves. He was the twelfth child of the headmaster of a great English public school, a curly-headed boy with wide nostrils, wide brown eyes, and a firm, well-shaped mouth. He was a good scholar, though less good than his older brothers, and far less good than his father expected him to be and believed he would be. Of a very scholarly family he was supremely, and more than a little rebelliously, the athlete.

He grew into a powerfully built young man, a little under six feet tall, weighing around a hundred and eighty pounds, small-footed, and very fast on his feet. He was a sprinter and broad jumper of considerable prowess and could play any game well, but he was at his best as an Association football player; one of the truly great amateurs at the time of the game's greatest amateur flowering. I still meet old *aficionados* of the game who remember his performances as a right-wing forward for the Corinthians, for Cambridge University, or for one of the great league teams that combined amateurs and professionals.

In the course of all this he managed to take honours in the Classical Tripos at Cambridge, and to publish a small volume of sonnets. Then he went on to become a schoolmaster. That he did so with conviction and dedication, I am quite sure; but I am equally sure that he would have chosen some other profession, probably that of soldiering, had it not been that in those days a commissioned officer needed private means to support him, while a schoolmaster did not.

Fortunately for him and also, as it turned out, for his country, he was able to combine soldiering with schoolmastering by joining the Territorials (the British Reserve Army), and by founding at his school the first cadet corps ever to enlist voluntarily every eligible member of the school. This I know was dedication, for my father believed, with at least a few others of his generation, that war was coming and that men should be ready for it. He believed, too, that war was unpleasant and deadly and should be avoided if possible; but he expected it to have compensations of excitement and fellowship and even glory; and nothing in him would ever have questioned a nation's right to expect her sons to fight and if necessary to lay down their lives for her.

So the pattern formed, for him and for thousands of others. A war might lie somewhere ahead of them, as other wars had lain in wait for other young men before them; with it would come sacrifice, gallantry, perhaps death, certainly victory and stronger statement of the values they believed in.

This was no grim shadow over the life of Edwardian England or even over Europe of the first decade of the century. Life was vigorous and creative and men lived it to the full without fear. My father was on duty at his school from seven-fifteen each morning. He coached all forms of athletics, gave special courses in English to the senior classes, ran the cadet corps with enormous thoroughness, and still found time for intense pursuit of two dearest interests: sports, by which he meant fishing and shooting, and freelance writing.

This pattern of his life was set before he was married and he held to it through the years until 1914, when the war started. We lived in a brick house among farm fields about four miles away from the school, which was at the top of a high hill. Every morning, summer or winter, my father rode those four miles on a bicycle. He was never once late for his seven-fifteen class, in fact it was his boast that he was never less than five minutes early for it. And he never missed a day for sickness. He found the daily uphill ride interesting and pleasant, and even argued that his magnificent health was in no small measure due to it; this I know, as I know many other things about him, from an article he wrote – in this case for *The Cyclists' Touring Club Gazette*.

His days at the school must have been full ones, but he found time to organize and run a small shooting syndicate among the masters of the school, and to train some of the boys as gamekeepers, beaters, and ferret-handlers; to stock a small pond on the school property with rainbow trout; and to train a succession of school rifle teams that won the highest competitive awards at Bisley.

He was home before supper time on most days, and it was then, and in the early mornings before he went to school, that I had a chance to know him. In the mornings I could come into the room where he was dressing and we would arrange it as a steeplechase course to train me for the day when I should be a runner. From the bed to a brown velvet-een-covered armchair was the brook; one landed at the far side, which was the chair, hands grasping the bank, body in

29

icy water to the waist; then clambered out and went on. He laughed a lot at such times and always thought up better obstacles; but he made me feel that the practice was serious and important and would one day be put to use.

In the evening, when he came home, I could fetch his slippers, which I was proud and happy to do. They were true carpet slippers, sloppy and worn, and they were kept in a box that made one end of the copper fender at the study fireplace. The box had a green leather upholstered top and was lined with green baize. It had a strong and distinctive smell, which I think was compounded of the resinous woods sometimes kept in it and the polish that was used to shine the metal of the fender.

The slippers were, I suppose, the deliberate resolve of an active man to be static and comfortable, and perhaps also in some Victorian tradition of masculine privilege. But they by no means signalled the end of his day's activities. On the luckier evenings he had time to teach me to aim and dry shoot a small bolt action rifle or (a most intense and vivid pleasure) help him change lines on fishing reels or sort trout flies. More often I spent my time leafing through the handsomely illustrated sporting books that were the back-bone of his library, while he settled at the roll-top desk to write. I realize now that he must nearly always have written again after supper, until late at night, to achieve his yearly output of two or three hundred poems and articles published in every conceivable type of periodical from *Boy's Realm*, through the *Evening News* and the *Daily Mail*, to the *Times*, the literary gazettes, and the great sporting magazines.

It is through this mass of journalistic effort and his three short books that I feel I know my father best. My mother has often told me of him that "he never grew up." His writing is all striving. It is easy and clear and graceful, beautifully phrased and convincingly argued. Much of it is on sporting subjects – shooting, fishing, football, or athletics. Some is military, some is serious consideration of educational problems, a few articles and poems are political, one or two of them violently controversial; a few, very few, deal with love and human relationships. The sum of them is a young man, who wanted to become a writer, who had the power and skill to write well, but never grew into the full measure of what he wanted to say or found the forms best suited to him. I know this because I have been through the years of striving and searching myself and still have not passed beyond them.

It may be that my father was primarily a man of action, that he never would have developed the powers of humanistic and introspective thought that make a great writer. Certainly the powers that showed in him most strongly were those of leadership, inspiration, and organization. He used them successfully in his everyday work at the school, so successfully that he was offered the headship of another great school in his early thirties. And he used them to still greater effect during the war years when he raised, trained, and finally led into action, a succession of "football" battalions. It is difficult not to believe that, had he survived, the experience of those war years and the intense relationships with other men, would have matured the man of action into a thinker and writer of rich humanity. But vision here is inevitably clouded by a son's almost paternal hopes for the unrealizable future of his father.

My mother has often told me, too, with a mixture of pride and exasperation, that my father "was a very conceited man," adding almost in the same breath: "I wouldn't give a penny for a man who wasn't." Mother herself was intensely and far too humbly modest. "I used to tell him," she said: "Alan, don't be such a conceited ass." Again, I do not doubt my mother's judgment for a moment, nor the wisdom of her tolerance. My father had what the sportswriters of today call "colour"; had it and used it as do nearly all good athletes and great leaders. One sportswriter wrote of his first appearance in big-time football: "Splendidly built, tremendously speedy, and self-possessed withal, he showed great dash and performed miracles on the right wing."

But if he managed to give this impression to others, he could also be thoroughly critical of himself. He wrote of an important game in which he played at about the same time: "I played disgracefully." And his self-possession by no means reflected a phlegmatic disposition, for he wrote of his first appearance before a crowd of fifty or sixty thousand spectators: "I remember I was the first to come out of the dressing room onto the field, but I turned tail and let someone else take the lead when I saw that sea of faces."

He wore, every day in the year when he could get one, a white carnation in his button hole. He was as careful of the appearance of his hands as a surgeon or a girl. He was proud of his body as only an athlete can be, and fanatical to the point of superstition in guarding its health; he would never lick a postage stamp, or open a letter except by cutting the flap, for fear of germs; he believed the dye in black socks was poisonous and would never wear them; he held firmly that drinking tea and eating fresh meat together set up a poisonous reaction; and no doubt he had a dozen other such minor fads of which I know nothing. They were symbols of his deeply honest conviction that for a man to abuse his body was a sin against his God, his country, and his family. So far as I know he was never sick for a day in his life, and he came through the years of trench warfare until his death with only a week out for shell shock and a minor wound.

This conceit, this pride of body that gives every movement a calculated grace, this self-possession that will not reveal or yield to the gravest doubts or fears, were all qualities that he used deliberately in action. After he was killed, his men wrote of him as "full of humour," "always cheerful," "just and considerate in and out of the line," and they refer again and again to the battalion under him as "one happy family." These things, which are the true heart and soul of soldiering

at combat level, grew from much more than surface performance. But men conditioned by such performance can always
find another ounce of inspiration in the seeming trivialities of
colourful leadership. These my father provided in large and
small degree; he wore yellow chamois gloves in combat, and
smoked his cigarettes through a nine-inch tortoiseshell
holder – these things, and the poise of his body under fire
have been remembered and told to me. Once, in preparation
for a surprise crossing of the Piave River in the Italian cam-
paign, he had the men he took with him grease their bodies
daily for a week. That also was remembered, as was the success of the crossing.

In the summer of the year before the war started, I was
five years old, old enough to go fishing with my father occasionally, and to carry a landing net. Once he knelt beside the
stream, covered a rising trout with his fly and hooked it. He
handed the rod to me immediately, whispered tense instruc-
tions and, at the first possible opportunity, slipped the net
under the fish and lifted it out of the water. We knelt together
on the bank over fish and net while he freed the hook. When
it was free he held up the fish. "There," he said. "Your first
fish. Hooked, played, and landed all on your own."

That was a moment when he was with me and I was with
him. There were not many of those, for a powerful and
energetic man in the full prime of his physical vigour has little
time to wait for the hesitant body of a five-year-old boy, even
if that boy is his son. But I remember another. During the
first year of the war, when he was still at home training men,
I had a uniform and a duty; the duty was to stand at our gate
and salute any body of troops that passed by. In the field
beside the gate I had an old sheet raised on a pole as a tent.
One day it was stolen.

About a week later my father woke me very early in the
morning. We dressed, both of us in uniform, and went out of
the house. In the field beside the gate, a full company of
soldiers was drawn up. Two or three officers came forward,

saluted, and spoke with my father. Then I saw the green pup-tent, already pitched where my old sheet had hung on its pole. While I was still realizing it was mine, given me by this full company of men, my father whispered: "You'll have to make a speech. I'll tell you what to say."

We stood together, on a weedgrown pile of old bricks. My father bent close to my ear and whispered: "Officers and men of "C" Company, Thirteenth Royal Fusiliers," and I heard my voice repeat the words after him. The rest of the speech is lost to me, as surely as my thin, boy's voice must have been lost on the morning air not fifty feet from where we stood. But I knew even then it was another time when he had waited for me and I had been with him.

In February of 1918, just a month before he was killed, his battalion moved from Italy to France, and he had a weekend leave in England. It was my birthday and he bought me an air rifle. I took it out into the backyard and shot with it for a whole morning without making a respectable target, though I reduced the range again and again. Finally I set up a new target and pumped ten shots into the bull's-eye from an inch or two away, then took it in to show him so that he would not be ashamed of me. He examined the target and admired it, made me aim the rifle and press the trigger in dry shooting, and praised me for my steadiness. He must have known then, as I remember now, that the rifle, even without my frailty, was incapable of such accuracy at a range of more than a few inches. So also with the trout that he claimed for me; he knew, as I remember now, nearly forty years later, that it was not mine but his. He hated and despised a lie or a false claim or anything won by subterfuge. I can remember or learn of nothing else that he let go in this way, either in himself or in anyone else, nor can I find a reason for it except that one of the dearest hopes of his heart was that I should follow his love of shooting and fishing. Once I thought it weakness in him; now I think it a gentleness above strength.

This was the man who wrote: "I have taken part in a great

34

variety of games and won in them my little successes, but they leave me cold, stone cold. A litter of spaniel puppies quickens my heart more than a university match; the emerald of a teal's wing, the bronze of a pheasant's breast, attracts more intensely than any deft juggling with an inanimate ball."

And in another mood, to "Love's Coming": "Will she come when the golden sunshine is kissing the poppy-clad lea? / Will she come when the silver moonbeams are dancing over the sea? / When winter is wearing for springtime a bridal robe of snow, / Or the fostering breath of summer is bidding her rosebuds blow? / Be it summer, spring or winter, be it dawn or at dead of night, / She will melt life's clouds with sunshine, flood its darkness with glittering light."

And yet again, with a gentle humour, almost prophetic, in the concluding lines of a sonnet to the cock pheasant: "For all your luxurious habits and ways / We have nothing to give you but honour and praise, / For, when you are done for, your epitaph reads: / 'Killed in action' – a better one, nobody needs."

So little, so little can I write in this piecemeal picture of a man I never knew, a man who lived in a different age than mine, in a different country and in far different ways. I have deeply missed knowing him and the riddle of what his life might have been will always puzzle me. Yet I do not regret the end for which he was so well prepared, nor do I forget that the actions of his last hours rallied thousands of men and saved hundreds of lives on one of the darkest days of a bitter war.

I have had sometimes to strive against the memory of his life and death, to win identification for myself against his powerful shadow. In doing so I have tested and retested, with almost savage harshness, the things he thought and did and believed in. Some few, superficial, and trivial things, I have been able to discard. The others, shaped to new times and new ways, are alive in me still and guide me as much as they guided him. Some things are truer than change; their meaning only strengthens and grows in change. My father held, for instance, that it was a mistaken loyalty to play for a league or school team when called upon to play on an international team. In the same way, he believed that in peace or war a man's country had the first and only inescapable call upon his services. I believe that in this day and age his unwavering patriotism would recognize a still higher loyalty, whose shape is only beginning to be clear.

4

Hardy's Dorset

(1957)

Thomas Hardy was born at Bockhampton, near Dorchester, in 1840, the son of a small but prosperous building contractor. My maternal grandfather, Alfred Pope, was born two years later, a few miles on the other side of Dorchester, the son of a small but prosperous farmer. Both the Hardys and the Popes were old Dorset families. Both sets of parents were ambitious for their sons, and the times favoured the ambitious parents of bright boys.

Logically, Hardy should have been sent to Dorchester Grammar School, which was founded by another Thomas Hardy, a direct ancestor, in 1569. He was sent instead to a small day-school in Dorchester, run by a fine scholar named Isaac Glandfield Last – because, says the second Mrs. Hardy, "the Grammar-school founded by his namesake was reported to be indifferent just then." Indifferent or not, my grandfather was sent there, and *his* biographer records that it was "in the palmy time of the old school under the Rev. Thomas Ratsey Maskew, M.A." Both boys did well in school, though it is said that Hardy was inclined to be lazy, which I strongly suspect my grandfather was not. On leaving school, Hardy was apprenticed to an architect in Dorchester, while Grandfather was articled to a solicitor in Bath. Both young men went to London to complete their professional training and were there at the same time in the middle 1860s. Probably, they knew each other there. Men from the counties clung closely together in London at that time, and both these later became members and officers in "the Society of Dorset Men in London."

Hardy was a good and successful architect, but literature was never far from his thoughts. He went about his work with poetry in his mind – and often a half-finished poem in his pocket. He read with enormous enthusiasm Homer, Virgil, Horace, and the Greek dramatists as well as Thackeray, Trollope, Moore, J.H. Newman, and other contemporaries, to the point where even he became concerned that he was neglecting his proper studies. On idle days in the office he delivered impromptu lectures on poets and poetry to the other pupils and assistants. And in the evenings he attended plays and operas whenever he had the price – or rather the half-price that was allowed to those who came to the theatre after nine o'clock.

Several of my uncles – for Grandfather's future held no less than eleven sons – have hinted that his London days were not without their very gay moments. Remembering the vigour that made Grandfather a force to be reckoned with even at ninety, I can well believe it. But, by the same memory, I doubt if gaiety was ever allowed to interfere seriously with self-improvement and professional studies. In the words of that day and this, Grandfather was a practical man, a very practical man, while Hardy was "something of a dreamer."

Both young men returned to their native Dorset in 1867, and both in due course forsook the professions for which they had trained so long. It was in 1874 that Hardy became a professional writer. Previously, he had lost fifteen pounds on the publication of *Desperate Remedies*, sold all rights to *Under the Greenwood Tree* for thirty pounds, and made a modest success with *A Pair of Blue Eyes*, but had continued to work as an architect. Now, with *Far From the Madding Crowd* running as a serial in the Cornhill magazines and the *The Hand of Ethelberta* almost finished, the time for the change had come. In the same year, he married Emma Lavinia Gifford, the sister-in-law of a Cornish rector, whose church he had been restoring for the past four years.

Grandfather also was married in 1874, but to his second wife. His first wife, a daughter of George Rolph, Judge Advocate of Dundas, Ontario, had died in 1871, only two years after he married her. He continued to practice as a solicitor until 1880, then bought a partnership in the Dorchester brewery and took over its management. Grandfather, as I have said, was a very practical man and the brewery prospered. Grandfather became wealthy and a considerable owner of good Dorset land, the Wrackleford estates lying just to the northwest of Dorchester.

Hardy, in his infinitely more exacting calling, also prospered and, in 1885, he and his wife moved into Max Gate, the famous house he built on land bought from the Duchy of Cornwall. Eight years later, Grandfather, who had also bought land from the Duchy of Cornwall, built a large house of his own within a mile of Max Gate.

It would be easy to multiply the points at which these two widely dissimilar lives touched. In 1886, for instance, the year in which Hardy published *The Mayor of Casterbridge* in fiction, Grandfather became, for the second time, the Mayor of Casterbridge in fact. The two men met on boards and committees; one followed the other as chairman of the Board of Governors of Dorchester Grammar School; together they were made honorary vice-presidents of the Dorset County Museum. Each in his way most deeply loved the county of his birth and each in his own way expressed that love. Both men planted trees, which is a sure expression of love of the land – Hardy more than a thousand of them on the two acres around Max Gate, Grandfather more than three hundred thousand on his Wrackleford land. Both men searched and probed into the history and antiquities of the province – Grandfather to produce a severely practical book, *The Old Stone Crosses of Dorset*, and little papers, read before the antiquarian society, on ancient customs and such special matters as dewponds and avenues of the county; Hardy to transmute the dead leavings of history and the living ways of Dorset folk into those great, brooding books that reach beyond practical matters, beyond Dorset, and into the soul of man.

I think it is fair to say that the two men were friends in their later years, and found many common interests in the gossip of the county and its ancient lore. Towards the end of the First World War, Hardy wrote a short foreword for a privately printed book, recording the armed service of my grandfather's eleven sons and three sons-in-law. It is a typically Dorset foreword, touching upon the family history, naming the Dorset place names associated with it; there is a touch of philosopher's wonder at such unanimity of action; and a concluding novelist's paragraph: "These chronicles, even when they become musty with age, may be interesting not only to the descendants of the family, but to others who are not of their blood or name. It often has happened that an account of what befell particular individuals in unusual circumstances has conveyed a more vivid picture of those circumstances than a comprehensive view of them has been able to raise."

Grandfather's respect for Hardy, at least in these later years, was unbounded – and to me surprising. He was more given to demanding than offering respect, and his judgments generally were material rather than intellectual or spiritual. But when he spoke of Hardy there was a tenderness in his voice that I can remember at no other time. When he went to visit Hardy, he went with ceremony, calling in advance to know if he might come, walking the distance from his own house to Max Gate, as though on a pilgrimage, and usually taking some member of the family with him. I went more than once, but the time I remember most clearly was in April of 1924, when I was sixteen.

I wish now I had had the precocious sensitivity and perception, to say nothing of the later powers of total recall, that so many writers seem to have for the outstanding occurrences of their youth. I was awed and impressed, but neither observant nor perceptive. And I was probably the most inarticulate diarist who ever bothered to record anything. "Sixth April 1924," the small book says. "Went to see Thomas Hardy with Grandfather. Had quite a good day for Sunday."

At that time Grandfather was eighty-two, Hardy was eighty-four. Grandfather was to live to be ninety-two, Hardy to be eighty-eight. Yet neither of them seemed to me then, or seem now in recollection, to be very old men. Both were spare and short, perhaps five and a half feet tall. Grandfather was the straighter of the two, with a brown face, dark-brown eyes, a straight, formidable nose and a neatly trimmed white beard, almost Spanish in effect. His feet were very neat and small in highly polished boots; his clothes were perfectly brushed and pressed; a wide wing collar framed his beard and a pearl stickpin was centred in the wide four-in-hand below it. Beside him, Hardy seemed a very gentle, very quiet, very grey man. His suit was grey and rather baggy and his tie was blue under a rounded stiff collar; his hair and drooping moustache were white; his brow was very fine and broad, creased with horizontal wrinkles that curved up over each white, shaggy eyebrow; his eyes, when he looked at you, were very blue and very lively, and seemed to light up the faint red of his cheeks.

We had been invited to tea. I thought Max Gate, red brick hiding behind its high, red-brick wall and among the dark Austrian pines, rather an ugly house. But once inside, turning into the drawing room to the right of the small dark hallway, everything was suddenly light and beautiful. This was a sunny April afternoon. The bright starched chintzes of chairs and sofas caught the sunlight and echoed it back to the pale walls and the pictures on them. The tea things shone and the second Mrs. Hardy was concerned for Grandfather, while Hardy himself was easy and hospitable and quite talkative.

Through the short meal the two men talked the Dorset gossip I had listened to for so many years – who married whom and when, who was a Symons or a Sheridan, a Williams, a Lock, or a Foster, before she was married; whether old John Legh belonged to the Owermoigne, the Marnhull, or the Chilfrome branch of his family, and who was his mother. These things meant little to me, but to them they were full of meaning, summoning the ghosts of ancient scandals, the laughter of pretty lips, the bold lost eyes of Wessex men, who had adventured away from the land and never returned. This was the drama and life of the county through a hundred years and more, cleaned and carded to the warp and woof of the family names and place names; meaningless strands to outsiders, but a rich pattern of gloom or glory to those who understood.

After tea, Hardy showed us the portrait of himself, recently painted by Sargent, that was the real occasion of Grandfather's visit. Grandfather liked portraits and had sat for several himself, so his interest was keen and almost personal. For some reason I had expected Hardy to be offhand about the picture, perhaps deprecatory, at most neutral. Instead, he was delighted with it, pointing quite excitedly to its qualities, praising Sargent's skill and understanding of him. He seemed surprised and flattered that the great man should have wanted to paint him at all, and I am sure now that he was – that the portrait was really a fresh and welcome reminder that the stories and poems he had drawn from his native Wessex had life and power far beyond the narrow boundaries of that little corner of England.

Grandfather was not normally a considerate man, but I saw now that he was watching Hardy, whose enthusiasm had tired him a little. Mrs. Hardy was hovering a shade anxiously in the background. Grandfather said his goodbyes, promising to come again very soon, and we went out into the sunshine of the April afternoon.

So much then, and no more, I saw of Hardy, being sixteen and young in bodily strength, full of the future, caring little for the past or its old men. I have often thought since that I should have made more of it, that I should have gone back again and again and tried to learn something, for I lived for two more years within reach of Max Gate. But in fact I doubt that even young Boswell himself could have made very much of it; sixteen cannot reach over the years to eighty with any degree of understanding, nor can the wisdom and greatness of old age give very much of itself to the harsh and eager urgency of youth.

Yet the memory of Hardy and that April afternoon has never been very far away from me in all the years since. Hardy used to record little fragments of stories and people, heard in passing, in his diaries. Once he wrote of two Cornish people he met while working as an architect. "Mr. Symons accompanied us to the quarries. Mr. Symons did not think himself a native; he was only born there. Now Mrs. Symons *was* a native; her family had been there five hundred years." By this exacting standard, I am certainly not a Dorset man. Born in Sussex, schooled in Surrey and Hampshire, living in Dorset only through the holidays of those boarding school years, and with most of my life spent half the world away, Mr. Symons would certainly rate me an alien and a suspicious character. Yet I feel and have always felt a Dorset man's claim in Hardy.

Claiming him, I have been moved and perhaps a little guided by what he wrote from London to his sister Mary about Thackeray: "He is considered to be the greatest novelist of the day – looking at novel writing of the highest kind as a perfect and truthful representation of actual life. . . . Hence, because his novels stand so high as works of Art or Truth, they often have anything but an elevating tendency, and on that account are particularly unfitted for young people – from their very truthfulness." Hardy himself suffered much from this same truthfulness. Because of it his first novel, *The Poor Man and the Lady*, was never published; his second, *Desperate Remedies*, was ruined by a narrow-minded reviewer in the *Spectator*; Leslie Stephen asked him to tone down sections of *Far From the Madding Crowd*; and through his whole career as a novelist he was sure of misunderstanding by much of the public and savage attacks from reviewers.

But I have thought of Hardy most often in considering the differences between the country he knew so intimately and discovered so profoundly, and that in which I have chosen to live and write.

It is difficult for a Canadian or an American, who has not known England, to realize what a vast country it is, in terms of people and living, and lived upon land. Even Wessex is vast in these terms; even tiny Dorset, fifty miles long at its longest, thirty miles wide at its widest, is so enormous that a lifetime could not begin to use it up nor to search out its last recesses.

For the writer, for the novelist especially, there is more to know, more to understand, more to use in the thousand square miles of Dorset than in the three hundred and fifty thousand square miles of my home province. It is a different knowing and a different understanding, more intimate and intricate, immensely rich in human values and references, the perfect raw material for the novelist's yield.

In this part of Canada – and I would choose again to live and write here – one can walk the hills and know them, travel the valleys and know them also. The streams and lakes lie open and comprehensible as they seem on the map, and even the great mountains are to be known; what difficulties exist are the physical ones of brush and slope and weather. I have seen a forest fire run through a hundred square miles around my house and been able to name the few insignificant works of man affected by it. I have been lost in my country and wearied by it and overawed by it – but never more lost or wearied or overawed than a man of Hardy wandering upon Egdon Heath, for the mind of man has only its own capacity for weariness or awe. The people of my country, except for the Indians, whose memories and traditions we have destroyed, came here yesterday and many of them will be gone tomorrow with no more trace than a few mouldering boards under the second growth. The country has little time to mould them and they have little time for it, unless to build a dam or cut down a forest before they run for the cities.

Another Dorset writer, returning to his native country after five years in Africa, called it "a land where every sod was sacred, had covered up bones for the dead or engendered corn for the living." And this was the land of which Hardy wrote. It is a land of Celt and Saxon and Roman and Dane, a used and lived in land of chalk downs and narrow valleys, broad meadows, wild heaths, and wild sea coast. There are songs and dances lost among the hills, ancient arts still nourished and gloomy country superstititions cherished. Cottage gardens flower in the half-memory of dark murders and lonely suicides; a Hangman's Wood nestles on every hillside and a Lover's Lane winds through every draw, rarely innocent of other sin than loving. The haunt of past battles and rebellions, of ancient crime and cruelty, the shadow of witchcraft and forgotten religious rites marks the land everywhere and touches its people still.

All this is a richness that no new land and no young people can know. If it sounds a heavy tradition, weighted with gloom, it is not. Fear and tragedy, battle and sin, can exist and be remembered only where there is happiness to make them a contrast. Wessex is a lovely land and Dorset the loveliest part of it. Nowhere is there so much in so small a space – every fold of the hills hides some quiet town or quieter village; rutted side-roads lead between ancient hedges to lonely slate-roofed farms; the downs spread and roll among gorse and woodland to tiny valleys, each with its stream and its history. Fat meadows of Frome and Puddle and Stour nurse red cattle, and the land yields everywhere, as it has for a thousand years.

So rich is the land that only one place name of Hardy's lies in the part I know best, the six or eight miles between Caster-bridge and Chalk Newton-Scrimpton. Hardy scholars have said that the Scrimpton of "A Few Crusted Characters" is probably Grimstone but I know it is not. In Hardy's story, Aubrey Satchel arrived at Scrimpton Church with his bride, Jane, to be married one morning. Aubrey had taken a drop or two and the parson would have none of him. So Jane, to be sure of her man, asked the parson to lock them both in the church tower for an hour or two until things were right. The parson agreed, but he was a sporting man and remembered that hounds were meeting nearby. He took off with them and it proved a good scenting day; he forgot about poor Aubrey and his bride until the following morning. Shocked at the possibilities, he hurried to the church and found the young people dutifully waiting, ready to forgo the one-night honey-moon they had planned so that the impropriety might never be known.

A kindly little story and a happy ending. But Grimstone has no church and no church tower. Frampton, less than a mile away, which Hardy knew well because the Sheridans lived there, has both. And Frampton, not Grimstone, is Scrimp-ton.

And what of the land between Casterbridge and Scrimp-ton, between Dorchester and Frampton, which Hardy never had occasion to use! Let me name just a few of the names in it. Gaston Bridge, the Trough Bridge, Bradford Bridge, and Muckleford Bridge. Stratton, Grimstone, Muckleford, and Bradford Purcell for the villages; Newlands, Longwall, Tillywhim for a few of the woodlands; Frome and Wrackle for the rivers. Stratton Manor, Lock's Farm, Pigeon's Farm, Sidling Farm, and Stybie's Orchard. Yes, and a Lover's Lane and a Hangman's Copse and the massive remains of Roman and Saxon earthworks on Poundberry. Every gate, every hedge, every cart track and spinney and field, every pool on the rivers, every bend in the roads, has its name, because the land is lived in and used.

These are riches of association that build about living people to give them depth and their deeds meaning. It is humanity stamped upon the land and pressed back upon itself. When I lived in Dorset, I went often to fish for salmon below Bindon Mill, near Wool. To get there I crossed Wool Bridge, where the ghostly coach of the seventeenth-century D'Urbervilles is said to pass. And I looked unfailingly, with a sense of pity and sadness, towards Wellbridge House, where Tess spent her fearful bridal night, as thousands have done before me and since me and thousands will in the years to come. For Thomas Hardy nursed his own grey and gentle spirit, conceived in the land, upon the land. And he spread its richness abroad for people everywhere to feel and know.

5
Izaak Walton
His Friends and His Rivers
(1953)

When Walton published *The Compleat Angler*, he was sixty years old. He was a mature, wise, gentle fisherman, who had developed a calm and deeply philosophical attitude towards his sport. Reading his book, one imagines him a charming old man, a ready friend, not unlearned, yet quite simple and remote from the great world. And one is entitled to the opinion, for Walton himself says of his book: "... the whole Discourse is, or rather was, a picture of my own disposition; especially in such days and times as I have laid aside business. ... "

The qualification is an important one, for Walton was the intimate friend of some of the truly great minds of his time. A devout Protestant and staunch Royalist, he lived through some of the most troubled political and religious years of his nation's history. He was a craftsman and a businessman, of whose formal education we know little or nothing. Yet he wrote a lot of good and important things besides *The Compleat Angler*.

Altogether, it is dangerous to form too simple a picture of just what manner of man he was. Perhaps his capacity for friendship, based on a tranquil and tolerant nature and deep understanding, is the key to him. Unfailingly sincere he was; simple, he cannot have been.

So far as anyone knows, Walton was the son of unpretentious country folk, small landowners perhaps, in Staffordshire. He moved to London, as an apprentice ironmonger, when he was seventeen or eighteen, and was admitted to the guild as a full-fledged craftsman when he was twenty-five. For the next twenty or thirty years he carried on his trade, in small shops in or near Fleet Street, and found time to build the experience from which he wrote *The Compleat Angler*.

It is tempting to wonder just what manner of store he kept and what manner of iron he wrought. Did he, perhaps, forge fish hooks, the Pennells and Limericks and offsets of his day? Was he the original prototype of the hardware-sporting goods dealer of North America? There is no direct evidence of this, yet it was in his business years that he entered into close friendship with some of the great men of his day, several of whom are known to have been keen anglers. In his little store he would have made and sold such small things as hinges, locks, latches, and weathercocks. Occasionally he may have undertaken larger work, such as wrought-iron gates or railings.

In *The Compleat Angler*, Walton puts little emphasis on tackle, but this is natural enough, for his tackle was quite simple, and he had advanced far beyond the youthful stage where enthusiasm for tackle almost obscures angling itself. There can be no doubt that he had more practical skill with his hands than most of his friends, or that he was able to help them in many little mechanical problems. Walton was a thirty-year-old ironmonger, with strong literary interests, and with growing skill and experience in the art of angling.

Among Walton's closest friends during his business years were several who were twenty or thirty years older than he, and who died nearly fifty years before him. Sir Henry Wotton was an ambassador and poet, Provost of Eton College, a famous man and an angler. Dr. John Donne, an enormously popular preacher and a poet who powerfully influenced later poets, was so precociously brilliant that he entered Oxford at eleven years of age. He was known as a difficult and exacting man, yet Walton became his intimate and adoring friend. He was also an angler. Michael Drayton, often known as the river poet, was an intimate of Shakespeare and Ben Johnson as well as Walton, and he too must surely have been an angler. John Hales, scholar and fellow of Eton College, known as "one of the clearest heads in Christendom," was Walton's friend, and fished with him.

It requires no stretch of the imagination to see such men meeting in Walton's shop to discuss with him literary, political, and religious affairs of the day, forgetting his comparative youth as they drew upon the reserves of faith and cheerfulness that were so strongly in him. It may have been they were attracted a little by the chance to pick over a batch of hooks, fresh from the forge, or test out a new rod butt bound with hoops of iron. Certainly there would have been some seventeenth-century equivalent of "The Thames is hot right now, out by Waltham Cross," and envious attention to Walton's accounts of great fish hooked on his latest trip to the wilds of Staffordshire or Derbyshire.

These men were men of the world, involved in large affairs and not without strenuous ambitions. The times they lived in were difficult and dangerous times for men of ideas and ambition. Donne had been in prison and had known extreme poverty. John Hales was thrown out of his fellowship at Eton for refusing to take a seventeenth-century loyalty oath and died in poverty. Sir Henry Wotton once fell into severe disfavour during his foreign service, and was arrested for debt when he was Provost of Eton. Drayton had seen the whole edition of his first volume of poems destroyed by order of the Archbishop of Canterbury.

It was a harsh time in which to think vigorously, but Walton had standards of religious faith and earthly loyalty

50

that seemed to grow stronger all through his life. He knew, perhaps more fully than any other man ever has, the sources of fulfillment and freshness that were to be found in the countryside and in his gentle art. No doubt he talked as easily and gracefully as he wrote. It is not very difficult to believe that his powerful friends found him at once stronger and more rewarding, surer in his assessments of life and living, than they were themselves. And it is unlikely that ever, in all their discourses together, they could have suspected him of a false or insincere word.

Donne, Drayton, and Herbert all died before Walton was forty. Sir Henry Wotton went not long after them. They left Walton, with other friends, to live on into far more troubled times of revolution and religious persecution. For all his serenity and strength, Walton must have been forced to test and search his conscience many times.

In 1649, he saw his king executed. He himself was living in Clerkenwell, only a few doors from Cromwell's house, where the death warrant is said to have been signed. In 1651, at the time of the Battle of Worcester, and only two years before *The Angler* was first published, he was in Stafford, no doubt quietly fishing the Sow and the Trent. Shortly after the battle he visited a Mr. Milward, a Royalist friend, who was imprisoned in Stafford. Milward handed to Walton a ring known as the lesser George, which belonged to the King, and asked him to deliver it to Colonel Blague, who was imprisoned in the Tower of London. Walton did exactly that, and Blague escaped from the tower and returned the Lesser George to the King in France.

To understand the full meaning of this, it is necessary to remember the importance that men of those days set upon such symbols of office and power. Cromwell's regime deliberately destroyed the ancient crowns of England, including St. Edward's crown, as though by so doing the return of kings could be prevented. Nearly forty years later, the last despairing act of Judge Jefferies, after the abdication of

51

James II, was to throw the privy seal into the Thames. Men were hung, drawn and quartered for far more trivial offences than Walton's. Yet it is certain he went about it with a calm mind and conscience, secure in the conviction that what he did was right and necessary.

One wonders what precautions he took, for he must have been known as a Royalist. It would be satisfying to believe he went out beside the Thames with grasshopper or minnow (the latter by preference, for Thames trout are big and hard to persuade) and caught himself a great trout. Then, having dressed it as he dressed the chub, "making the hole as little and near to the gills as you conveniently may," he slipped the Lesser George into the fish's belly and carried it safely to his friend the colonel in the Tower. But it seems more likely that, secure in the armour of a clear conscience and a simple courage, he just walked through the guards with the jewel in his pocket.

This is sometimes referred to as "the only known adventure" in Walton's long, quiet life. Yet clearly it was not. Having the friends he had, holding the beliefs he held, he must often have been in danger. It is known that he moved from Chancery Lane, in 1644, because it was "dangerous for honest men to be there." We know, too, that many of his friends, perhaps the majority of them, were highly placed churchmen, at a time when churchmen were always in trouble.

Two years after *The Compleat Angler* was first published, there was much religious persecution, and the clergy were banished from London. Walton quietly records that he met Bishop Sanderson in London that year "in sad-coloured clothes" and spent an hour with him in a tavern where "he made to me many useful observations of the present times, with much clearness and conscientious freedom." Some of the conversation is recorded in Walton's *Life of Sanderson*, and the words were directly against recent state orders and against "the unhappy Covenant . . . brought amongst us." If we know of these two incidents through records so casual as to have been little more than chance, plainly there must have been others.

Yet Walton, for all his convictions, was truly a quiet and inoffensive man, too deeply sincere ever to look for glory, too honest a Christian ever to provoke trouble, too calm and reasonable ever to be contentious. In this at least, we may safely trust his book's picture of his own disposition. His choice of rivers, his choice of angling methods and ways, closely matched the happy serenity of his character.

There is little doubt that Walton was a great walker, as must have been most of the anglers of his day. It has been suggested that he kept a horse in London and rode it out to his fishing. But, even so, he must often have walked. He is walking when he meets the fowler and hunter of his book, and they walk for many a mile after the meeting. Walton thinks nothing of a mile or three or four along the stream to a favourite fishing place: "We are not yet come to a likely place; I must walk a mile yet before I begin." But I think he walked them easily and companionably, talking if he was with friends, looking about him and noting everything if he was alone. He was happiest wth quiet streams and quiet fishing, though Cotton taught him to love the wilder Dove, and he himself wrote of Hampshire, which he knew well: "I think [it] exceeds all England for swift, shallow, clear and pleasant Brooks, and store of Trouts . . . ."

Much of *The Angler* is written of the Lea, near Waltham Cross and Tottenham and Ware. In Walton's day it was a wonderful stream, wandering gently among lovely meadows, with "primrose banks" and "honeysuckle hedges" to sit down upon or under, altogether a perfect place for Walton's method of catching a trout on a hot summer evening. "Get a grasshopper, put it on your hook, with your line about two yards long, standing behind a bush or a tree where his hole is, and make your bait stir up and down on the top of the water." A good place, too, for drifting quill or cork over a quiet, smooth roach "swim," or for leaving a rod to fish for itself, which, Walton says, is "like putting money to use; for they both work for the owners when they do nothing but sleep, eat or rejoice...."

But even in Walton's time industrialization of the Lea had begun. Sir Hugh Mydleton's canal was in course of construction; much building followed it, and then pollution. The charm of the countryside is largely gone, and little of the stream would now be recognizable to Walton, though the river still holds a fair supply of coarse fish and an occasional trout.

Like the Lea, the Trent, river of Staffordshire, Walton's home county, has been greatly changed since his time by industrialization and pollution. Once "the most famous coarse fishery in England and a salmon river of value," it has been slowly restored in this century to produce fair fishing, which is still improving. Its tributary, the Sow, which flowed through Walton's property at Shallowford, and where he may have fished as a boy as well as in later life, is now preserved by an anglers' association, and holds perch, pike, roach, chub, dace, and trout – an assortment that could hardly have been exceeded in the seventeenth century.

Walton fished the Thames, even as many of his followers fish it today. It is changed, of course, perhaps in many places beyond his recognition. But one place he would surely know: the bend below the playing fields at Eton, called "Black Potts," where he fished through many an afternoon with Wotton and John Hales. There are chub there still, and roach and dace and pike, perhaps even a fine trout or two. For the Thames still yields some enormous browns to a devoted fraternity of Thames Trouters.

The Kentish Stour still holds sea trout, but whether they are the great "Fordidge trout" of which Walton wrote I do not know. Walton called them "the rarest of fish, many of them near the bigness of a salmon, but known by their different colour; and in their best season they cut very white." If they were rare in Walton's day, perhaps they are still rare – but not unknown.

Walton spent much of the last thirty years of his life near Winchester. He worked quietly on his *Lives,* and certainly fished as keenly as ever. Marston imagines him on the Itchen, near Shawford, and I certainly hope it was so, for the Itchen is a lovely stream, full of trout and grayling. Walton would have hunted them with worm or minnow or grasshopper, as the season directed; but no doubt he fished the natural mayfly when the big ephemera was up, dapping it skilfully over the deep pools, wafting it ahead of him on the wind over the shallows. And he must have tried, often enough, the wet-fly techniques he would have learned from Cotton on the Dove.

The Itchen is still a fine trout stream, broad and clear and weedy, one of the classic dry-fly streams of England. I saw fine trout rising freely along it during the war years, and once, as I crossed a footbridge near Shawford, I knelt and scooped up a great swatch of weed that was caught there. It was crawling with handsome, healthy fresh-water shrimps, pale grey and brilliant, the sure abundance of feed that grows big trout. It is not unlikely that the Itchen today, like the Test and a few other well-preserved south-country chalkstreams, holds more trout and bigger trout than in Walton's time.

I have said little of Charles Cotton and his Derbyshire Dove. Cotton was thirty-seven years junior to Walton, who had been a friend of his father. He was traveller, soldier, poet, courtier, and man of the world, yet a dear and close friend of Walton's later years. Cotton was full of Walton's own sincerity and gentleness and friendliness, and Walton must have found him a refreshing and enlivening companion.

Cotton's stream, the Dove, is, like Cotton himself, lively and strong and bright, carrying the wildness of the Derbyshire hills. Walton travelled north to visit his friend, perhaps to discuss with him the great translation of Montaigne that

Cotton was later to undertake, certainly to fish and to discuss Cotton's addition to *The Compleat Angler,* which was published with the fifth edition in 1676. It is the most famous friendship in the history of angling, and one of the most touching of all times.

In 1674, Cotton built the little square fishing house on the banks of the Dove that is the true shrine and tabernacle of modern anglers, with its famous interlacing of initials I.W. and C.C. over the doorway, and the inscription "Piscatoribus Sacrum, 1674." The fishing house has been through many vicissitudes and restorations, yet it stands today with the exterior just as it was in Cotton's time. I hope it will always so stand, sacred to fishermen and especially to the memory of two fishermen. There is reason to believe that it will, for, with much of Dovedale, it is now the property of the National Trust of Great Britain.

As for the Dove itself, the footbridge and the slippery cobblestones are gone. Little stone weirs across the stream are new. Pikes Pool is unchanged, with the tall rock still breaking the water, and all the essential beauties of the stream and its valley are as they were. Walton and Cotton would recognize the beloved place, notice the changes, and be well pleased by the gentle treatment of almost three centuries. May all anglers and very honest men find the way there once before they die.

6

The Writer in Isolation
A Surprised Exploration of a Given Subject
(1959)

There cannot be, for a writer or for any other man, complete isolation. He will not find it in a monastery, nor in a hermitage, nor even in the careful architecture of some retreat especially designed towards that state. Influences are everywhere and the very fact of withdrawal, if he attempted it, would be in itself a most powerful influence. A writer is, by definition almost, a man sensitive to influences; he may reject them or accept them, search for them or flee from them, but he cannot be neutral or unfeeling about all of them.

The isolation of my title, then, is something at once less and more than the impossibility of withdrawal. It has no special reference to the "social consciousness" that was considered essential by many writers and critics of the Depression years, nor to the "engagement" of post-war writers, especially Europeans. It simply refers to the writer who, by accident or design, has placed himself and done his work largely beyond the reach of intellectual groups or associations. How does it work out? Is it good or bad, satisfying or disappointing, confining or broadening? If a deliberate choice, does it serve a useful purpose? If accidental, does it lead to frustration and indifferent work?

Absolute isolation from outside intellectual and artistic influence should produce that rather vague being, the primitive. But true primitives are rare creatures in a time of universal literacy; a painter or a musician absolutely without academic training or sophisticated influence is a possibility; but a writer's basic skills are taught in school and no one with literary inclinations, even though they may be dormant, is likely to evade all acquaintance with the writing of the ages. So a writer's isolation is likely to be qualified almost from the beginning. Someone will have tried to teach him to write more or less acceptably in his own language, and he will have experienced in some measure the power and effect of good writing. If he has any natural skill and ability, this may well be enough to start them working for him.

Most young writers feel strong doubts about the quality and potential of their skill, as well they may. After all, anyone can write. Why should one man's writing be of value, another's worthless? Where is there a test, whence can come the beginning of self-confidence? Where can be found the assistance or instruction that will transmute ordinary writing into writer's writing?

The natural answer to these doubts, and the almost inevitable fate of the urban writer, is association with other writers, established or aspiring. Nearly all artists turn to such associations at some stage of their careers. Some treat them lightly and casually, some take them very seriously and use them extensively. Some men become lost within the groups so formed, contributing much within them and nothing at all outside them; still others find refuge from their own incompetence in talk of art rather than artistic production; others again contribute greatly and produce strongly; others may pass quietly, almost unnoticed, and go on to become important artists or great patrons or businessmen or ditch diggers.

There is nothing very strange about this. All professions and interests tend to associate among their own kind and all such associations contribute more or less to their participants.

There have been some great and successful associations among artists – forced associations, such as that of the Impressionists, purposeful associations, such as the Group of Seven, deliberately chosen associations, such as that of the Pre-Raphaelites, natural associations, such as those of the eighteenth-century coffee houses, casual associations, such as those of Paris and Bloomsbury between the wars. Every capital and most large cities of the world breed them and have done so since the flowering of Athens. They are always of some importance to the individuals concerned and occasionally of importance to all civilization.

It is these associations that the writer in isolation denies himself, either deliberately or through force of circumstances. Does he gain or lose? Obviously it is an individual matter and can only be discussed in terms of individuals. And when I think it through, with a mind always faulty in recalling what little it has learned, I realize I do not know who were, or who were not, writers in isolation. Herman Melville, perhaps, and W.H. Hudson, Thomas Hardy, Kipling – but it won't really do; these men have been independent of groups and group influence, but they were not out of touch with other writers of their times. Thoreau seems like a lonely man, but he was never far from his group. Old Izaak Walton, simple and contemplative though he was, regularly foregathered with such noble minds as Henry Wotton, John Donne, John Hales, Michael Drayton, and Ben Jonson.

Among the artists, I think of Winslow Homer and, paradoxically, the Group of Seven. Why these? Because they set out to see a new continent through new eyes, cutting themselves off as best they could from academic theory, and they succeeded. But surely there had first been training, associations, discussion, and understanding of the older theories before a new theory could develop. They merely did what most artists of value do – they grew through associations and went out boldly into the isolation of maturity and production.

Consider, at the other end of the scale, those amateurs of

59

painting and literature who are to be found in almost every Canadian settlement, however small. A few are primitives, unashamed as Adam and Eve before the serpent gave them an interest in life, and their work should be protected from the light of day, with flaming swords if necessary. Most are in touch with others like themselves; they may grow alone and produce alone, but they are not really in intellectual isolation.

When the topic of this essay was suggested to me, I readily assumed that I had some claim to be considered a writer in isolation. Now I am very doubtful about the claim. I was raised in a stoutly philistine atmosphere of athletics and field sports, but it was broken by a number of good schoolteachers and by a good post-school tutor; it was broken, too, by the memory of a father and a grandfather who had written.

By the time I was eighteen, I had sold one or two short pieces of writing and was working in Pacific Coast logging camps. But I was not in isolation. For one thing, I read a good deal, and not altogether badly; for another, my companions nearly always knew that I had ambitions as a writer and did not hesitate to advise and guide me. I recall dozens, if not hundreds, of bunkhouse discussions not a fraction less intense, if possibly less recondite, than those of the most vigorous intellectual groups. My friends were realists to a man; they begged me to tell the truth, all the truth, not as poets and writers and film directors see it, but as they themselves saw it – the daily truth of hard work and danger, of great trees falling and great machines thundering, of molly hogans and buckle guys and long-splices. They made a profound impression.

In my early twenties I began to publish books and soon found myself on the fringes of intellectual groups – in London, Seattle, Vancouver. They were mixed groups generally; film and theatre people, a few writers, painters, musicians, and those non-practising amateurs of the arts who are often the strongest members of the groups. I contributed nothing that I can recall, invariably felt myself immature and insensitive, yet learned a good deal that removed me still further from the simplicity of isolation. Remembering my friends in the bunkhouses, I even became afraid of learning too much. I had a belief that if I could apply a straightforward mind to a wholly new country, then in some miraculous way the power of the pen would do the rest and produce literature. This was a conscious fear and a conscious belief, and both, I think even now, made some slight measure of sense. I was never very happy with the theories of the groups and felt no urgent need of them. But I wonder if I did not withdraw mainly because of a sense of my own deficiencies. I lacked the intellectual background, the depth of reading and the measure of artistic understanding necessary to take full part in such groups. Rather than face the problems of learning in public, I turned towards an isolation where I supposed I could learn for myself.

I wonder sometimes whether I might have become a better writer if I had talked and listened more to theories about art and writing. But it is a profitless wondering. I am not a person who takes kindly to groups. I mistrust, for myself, most theories of writing that do not fit with my own instincts about it. I feel that showing unpublished work to other writers not directly connected with its publication is a form of indecent exposure. I am fearful of too much close analysis of style and purpose, because I feel it may destroy both. And I believe too much talk before audiences, however small and select, wastes a writer's substance. Occasionally it may sharpen something in advance of the actual writing, but too often it simply defers the hard test of writing – sometimes forever.

Even in retreat from the fringes of my uncertain groups, I did not find, nor really seek, isolation. I married an intellectual, far better read and artistically far more sophisticated than myself. She has an untiring mind, which has grown steadily, and I have not been able to hide from it or run away. A hundred areas of thought and theory that might otherwise have remained closed have been opened to me; a dozen disciplines are there to test careless adventuring or shallow expression, a multitude of enthusiasms to stimulate and suggest. These are seldom spoken things or applied directly to the craft a writer must always ply alone; they are the simple outgrowth of living and companionship and by far the more powerful for that.

Few serious professionals, be they poets, novelists, or essayists, can afford to live and write in isolation from the science of their times, and I am no exception. Biologists, educators, lawyers, sociologists, psychologists, and a host of others expert in their various fields, have directed me with influences as hard and unshakable as those of my early bunkhouse mentors. It is true that they influence thoughts and conclusions rather than the techniques and emotions of writing, but this scarcely makes them less important or reduces their impact on the protective rim of isolation.

Lastly, there are the quiet and easy associations of maturity, the voices of those wise and experienced friends with whom one discusses many and deeper sympathies. These also are influences, fine shadings of influence that make larger differences than all the hot and anxious arguments of youth. Nothing, perhaps, is farther from isolation than these, no influence more subtly corrective.

It would be hard, I should think, for a writer of plays in English to live very far from London or New York. Producers, directors, actors, the very theatres themselves are all part of his life and his craft. Away from them, here on the shores of the Pacific Ocean, for instance, theatre itself seems less important, a remote and artificial medium instead of the lively and powerful one it really is in its proper setting. Film, radio, and television are less remote, but one still tends to approach them, if at all, as an outsider, a provincial. This, for the writer of books and verse and ordinary prose, is a beneficial isolation; he is largely spared the urgings and importunities and temptations of these other crafts.

But the writer of books and verse and ordinary prose is

never in any degree cut off from the excitements and discoveries and stimulations of his own craft. Books, reviews, and criticism are his for the reading and no man has the advantage of him in this because reading at its best, like writing, is a solitary affair. A book read in New York or New Denver is the same book and carries the same values for the same reader. Books alone, without radio or television or films, without groups or discussions or any other intrusion of man, totally destroy intellectual isolation. And this is a type of destruction that few writers are likely to feel any inclination to resist. Jamie Anderson, the fur trader's son, rhyming his Cariboo ballads in Barkerville during the gold rush, might have been a better poet if he had never heard of Robert Burns. On the other hand, he might not have written at all.

I have written of isolation as though it were at once highly desirable and completely unattainable. Neither suggestion is altogether accurate. As Domdaniel told Monica: ". . . creators must simply do what seems best to them. Some like solitude, some like a crowd." Some writers like to think slow thoughts and struggle with them alone; others like the brilliance and stimulation of constant intercourse with their peers. Neither is likely to produce poorer work for doing what he likes, or better work for doing what he hates.

I think I have been overly afraid of influence or possible interference with my natural inclinations and such natural ability as I have. I know now that neither of these things is easily shaken or distorted or perverted. Any writer who has the necessary minimum of integrity can readily afford to expose himself to influences of all kinds without fear of loss and with some real chance of gain. Yet talk is a danger to writers. More than that, talk is a positive, ugly menace. Talk is so much easier than writing, its satisfactions are so immediate, that some of the need to write is all too easily lost in it. It may be true that no man will talk himself out of being a writer if he has it in him to write, and no doubt some men have capacity for both. But I think the frustration of enforced

63

silence is good for most of us. Young writers who meet in groups to discuss their own work would be better at home writing more and talking not at all; and old writers who yield to the incessant demands of service clubs and other organizations are bleeding energy they need for the vastly more important business of writing. Even service club members can read if they would; and if they want a writer's words, the printed page is where to find them.

I have said nothing of the intrusion of economics upon isolation. They do intrude, as every professional knows. If communication is the purpose of writing, which I devoutly believe, the intrusion is not always vicious; it may even be a healthy discipline. Publishers, agents, and editors understand communication; their guidance is usually important and often artistically valuable. They can easily interfere too much, but the wise ones do not and the wise writer always knows where to draw the line of his treasured isolation, as surely as he knows when he can yield to economics without harm to his faiths. I have known moments of panic and despair at the thought that London and New York were thousands of miles away, but one weathers these. The mail serves somehow, the needed advance arrives, the commission is negotiated, the editorial doubts are resolved. And in the long run remoteness still serves a useful purpose. One is protected from easy dependence and from small interferences that do not travel easily by mail. Associations with publishers, agents, and editors are likely to be among the pleasantest and most satisfying a writer can have. But a measure of distance helps to preserve respect on both sides.

In the end, all writing is isolation. A man observes and absorbs readily enough among his friends. He may test ideas or sharpen argument or search for encouragement in talk. But he must mature his thought, develop and control his emotions, plan his work, alone. And he must write it alone.

Whatever measure of isolation I have known, I do not regret. Writing is the most natural of the arts because it stems directly from man's daily habit of using words to express his thoughts and emotions. Refinements of style and technique, sophistication of thought and approach, are desirable in their time and place. So also is freshness, sometimes even simplicity, of view and the impact of the uncluttered mind upon the ancient scene. Reconciling these two propositions is by no means the simplest of the large personal problems every writer must face. I believe some measure of isolation is helpful in this, but at the same time many outside influences must play their part. It would be as absurd for the novelist of 1960 to come to his craft in the same frame of reference as Richardson or Smollett or Fielding as for the automotive engineer to go to Leonardo for his ultimate refinements.

No man, not even the primitive, has ever written from a vacuum. There are always influences, sought or unsought, subtle or obvious, fundamental and superficial. A blade of grass or a city street, a fine mind or a rough one, friends or enemies, love or hate, joy or fear, reasoned argument or unfettered emotion, any or all of these things and many besides have made their impact upon the mind that guides the pen. Isolation can never be more than a matter of degree. It would be grossest ingratitude for me to deny my influences by claiming to have written always in isolation.

7
Writer's Notebook: Influences
(1953)

I doubt if any writer can name with certainty and accuracy the other writers who have influenced him, for some become lost in the ancient mists of his youth; others are confused by and tangled among the many other influences of adolescence; others again, and perhaps the most significant among them, may have been suppressed in the mind for one reason or another. My own wife tells me I like to deny all influence and boast that I sprang full-armed from the brow of Jove, which is a fair enough indication of how arrogant some of us become.

But in my rare moments of humility I can recognize some of the influences that have helped to shape both what I write about and how I write. From a very early age I remember some written words of my father's: "The sentimental aspect of natural history is wholly to be condemned as lacking in truth. I am not at one with those pseudo-naturalists who credit animals with all the fears, feelings, and sensations of ourselves, with the thoughts and reasoning powers of mankind; and who write of wild creatures as though they were human beings with human cares and worries." I accepted those words consciously and applied them faithfully as I read the animal stories of Thompson Seton, Charles Roberts,

John Fortescue, Percy Fitzpatrick, and many others. I read always with pleasure, often great pleasure, but far more critically than I should have without my father's comment. In all my youthful reading of animal stories I do not think there was one which satisfied me it had fully passed his test; and I resolved that I would one day fill the gap.

This is influence in its simplest, most direct and most recognizable form. Nothing else is as clear, because other and later influences were at once deeper and less precise. I read an infinity of sporting writers, both technical and literary. Technical writers such as Halford, Skues, Hutton, Sheringham, La Branche, Hewitt, and Francis Ward taught me much about fish and fishing and also opened my mind to how much more there was to learn about both; without them I could not possibly have had the curiosity to learn what little I have learned about northwest fish and wildlife. But at the same time I have always preferred the literary sporting writers, such men as Surtees and Nimrod and William Scrope, Hudson, Richard Jefferies, Grey of Fallodon, Plunket Greene. If I resolved at all upon the matter, consciously or subconsciously, I chose to follow these rather than the technicians.

If the number of times I read it during my sixteenth and seventeenth years means anything at all, I must have been influenced by Fitzgerald's *Rubaiyat*. But whatever it did was nothing compared to the excitements of George Meredith – the dark and feverish adolescence of Richard Feverel, the tormented beauty of Diana Merion; I knew even then that Dickens, or even Ainsworth, was a far more powerful fiction writer than Meredith, yet in Meredith I felt the power of fiction directly upon me personally; he was not merely a teller of stories, but a recorder of human passion and experience that could well be within my own immediate scope. I may never have written a word that was influenced by him, but I cannot forget the hours I spent with him.

As nearly as I can remember, the English poets whom I read most thoroughly at the impressionable time were

Milton, Wordsworth, Tennyson, Masefield, and Kipling, but the last three are inevitable youthful choices, because they were so often narrative poets. It seems to me, as I try to do it, enormously difficult to distinguish between a temporary literary preference and influence. Why do I name these? I read a hundred others in my teens and it would have been easy to substitute such names as Byron and Keats and Shelley, Blake and Morris, Hardy and Bridges. And why leave out Shakespeare, unless because he is too obvious? But if I am in debt to a wealth of English poets, as I know I am, I hope the major debt is to Milton, because none is greater.

There was a time when I tried to imitate the convincingly matter of fact storytelling style of Kipling, and another time when I reread Stevenson to teach myself the ease and grace that are his. But one cannot borrow in any such way as this; a style is made for a man and a time, not for another man in another time. I have read and still read the Russians – Tolstoi, Dostoyevsky, Turgenev – mainly for pleasure, but also because I believe them giants of literature, men from whom influence should come if it comes at all. In the same way I have read and still read Henry Fielding, Thomas Hardy, and many others only a little less obviously supreme. One could scarcely aim to be a writer and not read them. And I wonder if a writer who knows none of the novels I have named can fail to be influenced, at least indirectly, by them if he writes in the English language. For that matter, can anyone who speaks the language claim to be uninfluenced?

Without being too preoccupied with form, I have written a good deal in essays – I am, in fact, talking now in what is essentially an essay form. I have not especially wanted to do this; in fact, I have often tried quite hard to find a way around it, because publishers and magazine editors like to think the essay is as dead as hieroglyphics. My American publishers never dream of calling me an essayist, and so far as I know never allow the offending word to appear in any of their catalogues or publicity. Unfortunately the form, or my version of it, very often fits both what I want to say and the way I want to say it. On the whole, both critics and readers have been very kind to my offence – certainly none has appeared yet with shotgun or horsewhip – but my publishers assure me this is only because of their skill in not calling my essays what they are so dangerously like.

However that may be, I must admit to having read Addison and Steele and Hazlitt, and those gentler English essayists of more recent date, Charles Lamb, E.V. Knox, and Patrick Chalmers. I have probably been influenced by them a good deal, though I have consciously resisted much of their gentleness and, I hope, all of their whimsy. The youngest of them is of an older generation than mine and the ways of their generations are not the ways of mine.

Which brings me squarely against the point of contemporary influence. No matter how much a writer may wish to avoid it, he cannot, any more than he can avoid some influence from the authenticated giants who have preceded him. He is part of his time and will read in his time. He is affected by the events of his time, as the influential writers of his time are affected by them. To remain entirely uninfluenced would not only be impossible, it would be to remain outside of one's time.

My own influential contemporaries are not all strictly contemporary. That is, some of them wrote in another generation, or even removed by several generations, though their influence in many cases had its greatest impact after their earthly time. The farthest removed of these contemporaries are probably Herman Melville and Walt Whitman, both men of the last century, both influential in this. Next after them in time are James Joyce and, in lesser degree, Virginia Woolf and D.H. Lawrence. And within ten or twelve years of my own precise span are such writers as Hemingway, Dos Passos, Stephen Vincent Benét, John Steinbeck, Archie Binns, and Thomas Wolfe. There can hardly be a writer working today whose attitude and approach to his work has not been influenced by James Joyce, and there are few whose style has not been influenced by Hemingway. I am no exception to either rule.

All these, whether they be strong or weak, plain or obscured, are influences. I have absorbed incidentally rather than sought deliberately among them. Certainly there are many others of the same kind, perhaps equal in effect, which do not come readily to mind. It is a writer's business to be influenced or wrought upon by everything he sees or hears or feels or reads and to get it, if he can, into the pattern of his own thought. I have searched directly for guidance not from fiction writers and poets, but from critics and thinkers. To keep the list within bounds, let me limit it to contemporaries, and those whose influence I have felt most powerfully. They are: Edmund Wilson, Lionel Trilling, Judge Learned Hand, and E.B. White. To these four I believe I owe more than to anyone else. And at least three of them are still adding to my debt.

To be influenced is not always to be in debt. In the course of my working life it has been necessary for me to read many things that were far from literature and at times even to write in forms precise rather than emotional, and language more nearly code than English. For many years now I have read scientific and technical papers on fish and mammals and most forms of conservation, and for the past ten or twelve years I have read a good deal of law. Some legal judgments are written in noble language, but most law is indifferent writing, painfully designed to leave nothing to the imagination. Practically all scientific and technical papers are stiff and clumsy jargon, designed to protect the writer from saying or suggesting anything he has not proved, fully intelligible only to a fellow-scientist or technician. Perhaps the discipline of working his way through such language is of some value to a writer. Writing it himself can scarcely be other than harmful. I have written legal judgments and army reports and a fair number of papers and articles which, though not unfailingly scientific, were near enough to it to need some of the jargon, and all the stiffness of a formal report.

One does not do such things with impunity. The circuitous, protective phrases cling to the pen, and the cautious, protective habit continues to stifle the mind and clog the imagination long after the need has gone. I believe I can control such clumsiness now and keep the restraint out of my writing. But it is still an influence in the sum of influences, and I would need to be a far bolder critic of my own work than I am to say it is no longer detectable.

Special causes are another influence that thrust themselves upon writers almost as a matter of routine duty. Writers are articulate and they are easily stirred, so I suppose this is inevitable. There is really little time, and little surplus energy in a writer's life for special causes, unless they grow directly from personal convictions and the total attitude of his writing, and even then he will be spending time that would almost surely be better spent in advancing a new book or a new story. For a writer is seldom important to anyone as a crusader or a special pleader. His real importance is in the sum of experience that he can share through his writing and in the quality of what he shares. Many influences make up that sum and that quality. The wider and more numerous they are, the richer will be his yield, provided always that he has the art and skill to transmute them into new meaning.

8

How Important is Reading?
To the Canadian Library Association
(1955)

Not so many years ago I knew a wise old man who could not read or write. He was in his eighties then, a happy man who had lived a full life; but he regretted he had been born too soon for the British Education Act of 1870, which compelled all children to attend schools. His sisters, a little younger than himself, had been sent to school and he was acutely aware that they had access to a whole wide world of print that was denied him.

In thinking of reading it is important to remember the old man, watching the world with his keen old eyes, and they were very keen; unable to record what he saw, and he wanted very much to record it; unable to compare and expand his experience with the recorded experiences of others, and he wanted very much to do both these things. He might very well have been my grandfather; he lived in the same community through an almost exactly parallel span of years. It is not at all unreasonable, though it may not be very tactful, to ask anyone much over the age of forty: "Could your grandparents read?" The generalized answer is: "Probably, but by no means certainly." Take it one generation farther back and the answer changes to: "Possibly, but just as possibly not."

Books and reading have been one of the major factors in

human civilization for a very long time. But until quite recently most of the reading was done by a very few people. Now nearly everyone in North America can read, but comparatively few people read any more than they have to. Public libraries, cheap, well-produced books, mass circulation periodicals are all rather new things. The majority of people haven't yet got into the habit of using them.

Maybe they never will. Reading is quite difficult and quite exacting. It calls for imagination and a fair amount of intelligence. It is an exercise of something more than the simple senses and therefore an unnatural performance, considerably more complicated than looking at a picture or listening to a voice.

It is just as well to remember all these things in considering the importance or otherwise of books and reading. Importance and popularity are not necessarily the same thing at all. What is popular is not always bad and trivial, but it is quite likely to be. So the fact that only a few score thousand people read books, while scores of millions hang upon radio and television and films, is not necessarily a useful yardstick of relative importance and value.

Nor is it highly significant when university professors observe that a fair proportion of their freshman students have never read even a single book all the way through. Probably the grandparents of these children never learned to read at all and the parents may well have been no nearer university than elementary school. So the non-reading university freshman is a considerable advance, even though one may feel his parents and grandparents would have grasped opportunity rather more firmly. So also with the parents whose children will "read nothing but comic books." What do the parents themselves read? The pictures in *Life, Maclean's* Magazine and the easier parts of the daily newspaper? If so, the preoccupation of the children is not especially surprising, because reading is an acquired habit and most such habits are picked up around the home.

There is a widespread belief that reading, like chastity, sobriety, and most of the virtues, is on the decline, driven into it by radio, film, television, the phonograph, the tape recorder, and the printed photograph. This is a comforting belief for elderly moralists and all those who remember their own youth as far more upright and virtuous than it actually was. But the evidence is against it. There has never been a time when so many people were able to read. There has never been a time when books, good books, were so cheap and so readily available or so widely read. There have never before been so many libraries, so well staffed or so well equipped with books. There have never before been so many newspapers, so generally well served by widely scattered correspondents or with such prompt news coverage.

Newspapers are not reading in the sense I am mainly concerned with in the present discussion. They are reading for a specific purpose, current information, and the state of the world is such that current information has never been of more vital importance to the people of the world. Radio, television, even films, have all tried to compete in providing the public with current information, yet newspapers today can count on a greater army of readers than ever before. A newspaper is still, for most people, the only satisfactory way of learning what is going on.

If these three great means of expression and information, and they are truly great means of expression, cannot supplant newspapers, is it reasonable to suppose they are supplanting any other form of reading? There is, I suppose, some sort of a statistical answer to that. But, like most statistical answers, it cannot possibly matter. The real answer is in an examination of what reading does and what these other things do.

Civilization is accumulated knowledge. Without the written word there can be little or no accumulated knowledge. Without the printed word there can be no comprehensive spread of accumulated knowledge. This spread of real knowledge is the true function of books and reading.

When a writer sits down to write a book, he is a man alone with an idea. He takes time and slow thought and the urgency of his message, and of these, still alone, he compounds his book. It is the expression of an individual, sent forth to be shared by other individuals who take it to themselves, each alone and slowly, with thought and his own urgent need to share what the writer has to offer. The urgency that was put into the book may last for an hour or a day or two thousand years, but while it does last the reader can find it.

Radio, television, and film are altogether different. They are dependent upon complicated mechanical techniques, which age and date very rapidly. And even apart from this, they are purely ephemeral means of communication, setting their own pace, entirely beyond control of the user, forever lost to him the moment their time is spent. He cannot ponder them or turn back to them. He must depend upon the vivid impressions that remain with him, upon some intensity of thought or imagination snatched from the passing sounds and scenes. The eye and the ear can take in only so much, and that little is the measure of his field for reflection and considered judgment. This has always been true of the stage. One has only to remember how much of Shakespeare's enormous influence has been in the reading rather than the performance of his plays; and how many wise heads have found Shaw's prefaces more satisfying than his plays.

This is not for one moment to suggest that these great modern miracles of communication are without virtue. They do things that books cannot do, and they reach and touch enormous numbers of people who never have read and never will read a book. As often as not they carry with them some of the substance of books; even when they do not, they carry the influence of books, for a producer can hardly be a non-reader, even though a consumer may be. I am quite sure that these three mediums together have never deprived writers or publishers of a single reader. No one who could depend upon them solely or mainly for mental satisfaction is even a potential reader. But I am equally sure that they have created many new readers, by exciting taste and curiosity, and by sheer educational value. And as they develop in scope and sophistication and technical competence they will create many more.

Not that all is well with books and reading. It never has been and undoubtedly never will be. Once upon a time books were scarce and expensive and poorly printed; publishers were exploiters and writers starved. Writers still skip a few meals, but most of these other evils have been corrected. The greatest danger to writing and reading today is the mass market. Publication, whether of books or periodicals, has become big business, with all the inherent evils and limitations of big business.

The mass circulation periodical was created by advertising. No such thing existed before extravagant advertising, no such thing could continue in existence without extravagant advertising. Therefore, it represents not loss but gain. It has made readers out of non-readers and it gives them much that is good. Its faults are timidity and conformity. It dare not shock or extend its readers, it must not frighten them with abstract or deeply considered ideas, it must somehow catch and hold even the dullest mentality – or risk a reduction of the advertising rates. With so much at stake the mass circulation periodicals have naturally developed a solid insurance system; they are mainly staff-written or else edited into inoffensive inanity. The few literary magazines continue to struggle as they always had to before the days of mass literacy. While they may have a few more readers than they once did, they are faced with higher production standards and greatly increased costs; and for the most part they have remained "little" magazines, barely surviving or closely succeeding one another if they fail to survive. Though they may not seem so in the face of the mass circulation figures, the little magazines are probably just as important and just as widely read as they have ever been.

Book publishing has not come under the heavy hand of the advertiser, nor is it likely to. But, like the literary magazines, it has come squarely against high production costs and, like them, it has failed to reach significantly into the enormous new market of mass literacy. Higher costs mean increased risk in an always risky business, and in publishing this has meant increasing caution and timidity. As with the mass circulation periodicals, caution takes the form of relentless search for safe conformity. The old-time publisher's reader has now become an "editor," dedicated to the task of repeating old successes and reducing everything that comes before him to the same flat level of safety. It is a self-defeating process and for that reason, one hopes, a passing fashion. But it is a far greater danger to books and the future of books than are all the so-called competing means of communication.

The brighter side of the picture, and the best evidence of public desire for good reading, is in the success of the few honest efforts publishers have made to reach the great new market that universal literacy offers. The paperbound book in drugstores and cigar stores is one of the really big facts in North American culture during the past twenty years. The preponderance of detective stories and prurient titles means little against the fact that hundreds of thousands of people are buying and reading books. The progress to good and even weighty titles has been very rapid and names like Mentor and Anchor, and others mean reading of the highest quality, readily available at reasonable cost. Many problems in such publishing have still to be resolved, but there can be no turning back from it and at least one pattern of the future is clear enough. With books such as these, and the Penguin series from England, the hardcover Modern Library titles, and many other first-class reprints, the book buying public is better served than ever before.

One of the sad discoveries of the modern liberal has been that even though people may be given equal opportunities in education, they do not all become equally educated and intelligent. But in spite of this, universal education constantly produces more and more people who are capable of absorbing and using first-rate ideas. People of this sort will put increasing pressure on every form of entertainment and on every means of mental and spiritual growth; they certainly will not neglect reading.

Books have so long been a ready means of entertainment that we are inclined to accept and forget their special qualities. A book can be read for an hour, laid aside, and picked up again. It can be carried anywhere and read anywhere. A good book has a power of absorbing and enfolding the reader like a dream; it makes pictures and ideas, creates suspense, pity, love, laughter, or wonder; it unites the reader's mind with the writer's, yet leaves the imagination free to range and soar; and it does all these things with no machinery more complicated than printed words on a page.

The best books are individual expression, deeply considered, created under one man's control from start to finish. In this form they are by far the highest means of transmitting abstract ideas, in fullest scope and finest shade, without limitations of haste or compression or popular appeal. They can be received in the same way, quietly, reflectively, individually, with considered and reconsidered judgment. The greatest flights of the human mind can be fitted to the printed page and shared with other minds. So long as human beings are concerned with more than material things, so long as desire for individual growth is a characteristic of mankind, books will remain the most significant means of intellectual communication.

It is inconceivable that our present civilization could have grown without the Bible, both the Old Testament and the New, without Plato and Homer, without Chaucer and Shakespeare and Milton, without Cervantes and Tolstoi and Dickens. It is just as inconceivable that the full scope and content of all this creative thought could ever have been transmitted by film or radio or television.

The truth is, of course, that the great ideas and ideals of the human race have always been expressed in many ways. Music, painting, sculpture, with the ephemeral arts of singing, acting, and dancing, have all proved themselves powerful means of expression, often better fitted than words to carry some special weight of meaning or emotion. The new mechanical means of expression are not substitutes for these, any more than they are substitutes for the written word. Rather they are a projection, and sometimes an enhancement, of their use. Even words are used in many forms. Song was before books and song still has its place, even in the telling of stories. There are spoken words and words in verse and the words of the broadside and pamphlet, as well as words in books, and all have carried great messages. Perhaps it is easiest to imagine the spoken word, words of the poet reading his verses, of the statesman speaking, of the actor on the stage, replacing books and reading. All these can now be recorded and stored away as readily as books, to wait for need or mood. They have their place and value. But it is still true that the ear will not endure very much at a stretch. And it is slow – no more than one-third or one-fifth as fast as the eye on the printed page. What is written here to be read in ten minutes could not be well spoken in thirty minutes.

The power of human thought is infinite, yet human wisdom accumulates very slowly, only through infinite testing and sifting. There is no more precise and powerful way of recording and expressing thought than the written word, no surer means of testing it than by reading the written word. These would be reasons enough to be sure that books and reading will always remain the largest influence in any modern civilization that allows for growth of the human spirit. But it is also true that there is a human need to share experience even when it is not of overwhelming significance. This need is the root of all art, the bond between every artist and his audience. Experience is shared daily, in every communication between men. If all men were fully articulate it would be shared best by direct interchange between mind and mind. But no man is fully articulate. Speech stumbles, the thread of thought shifts and falters, interchange is rarely complete or perfect.

The written word has long been the answer to this failure of communication. The writer, imperfectly articulate though he may be, has trained his powers of expression and he inherits the techniques of two thousand years. Alone and over a long while he searches and refines his experience, whatever it may be, and commits it to paper, in exhortation or interpretation, in understanding or misunderstanding, in joy or sorrow or pity. The reader receives it, alone, with a quiet mind, in his own chosen time. He may accept or reject the writer's experience, but if the book is honest at all he will be stirred by it, made happy or unhappy, changed a little or increased a little by it. He will have shared experience with another under conditions as nearly ideal and complete as can be found.

This, ultimately, is the importance of books and reading. A man offers the best he can summon from himself to other men, and they are free to receive it in their own time, to turn away from it or go back to it. A few pieces of paper, sewn together and marked with signs, can convey thought, meaning, emotion, even the illusion of life itself. It is a miracle of communication, a direct reaching of mind to mind over time and space that has no equal. So long as men think and need to share thought, books will go on.

9

The Way into Books
To the American Library Association
(1961)

Samuel Johnson said that people who don't read "have nothing to think and very little to say." In its time that was a pretty harsh remark, because a very large number of people *couldn't* read. Today nearly everyone *can* read but Johnson would, I am sure, be very quick to point out that no greater proportion of them does read than did so in his day. The rest still end up with "nothing to think and very little to say."

Since this is so under modern conditions when people can read, I am inclined to think it is as it should be. Many people do not want to think and do not want to talk about anything that matters very much. And if they do not want to, why should they? But it remains important to give them the chance to make a positive decision about it – to show them what reading is and can be, and that having something to think and something to say can be quite pleasant when one gets used to it.

Johnson also said: "A man ought to read just as inclination leads him; for what he reads as a task will do him little good. A young man should read five hours in a day and so may acquire a great deal of knowledge." I find myself very much in sympathy with this statement. Reading should be very little guided from outside, and there must be plenty of it to do any good.

Children and young people should have a chance to read and, beyond that, a chance to know what reading can give them. If they then reject it, there is little more to be done. The question is: What is a chance to read and what constitutes a chance to find the joy and satisfaction of reading?

It is a mistake to separate books into nationalities. The best books do not so separate themselves: they are translated into many languages and read by many nationalities. Because they deal with universal things, they find echoes of experience in everyone. A local book or a national book may have some special value because it is closer to the experience of its readers, and for this reason it will become particularly desirable within a certain locality or nation. But while this value deserves recognition, perhaps especially for young people, it is important not to confuse it with greatness or even excellence. A book is good, bad, or indifferent in itself and not by means of its national origin.

It is very important to give young people a chance to understand, from the very start, that books are the products of men and women, not of nations, nor of factions, nor even of factories. I say this because of a recent experience with a group of elementary school children, who were brought to my study to see an author at work. The teacher explained that some of the books they had read had their start in this room. "Here?" asked one little girl. "You mean like this on the desk?" "Yes," said the teacher, "what did you think?" "Why," said the little girl, "I thought they made them up in factories."

The librarian must look out upon the whole of literature, upon world literature in the grand sense, as the realm that should be opened to the child. This is an attitude of mind rather than any immediate practical achievement. But only if the attitude is there, in full force and virtue, can the way be opened to the achievement.

In Canada, we do, of course, give special attention to Canadian books, and our children will naturally give them more than an even break. We want to see ourselves as our own countrymen see us. We want to read our own history as it reveals itself to a Canadian mind. We want to see our present and explore our future, examine our institutions, test our feelings, in the light of Canadian experience. Until recently all these things were luxuries we could barely afford. We are just beginning to recognize and realize a Canadian literature that fills many needs. This is a help, I am quite sure, both to librarians who would lead children into literature and to children who would find their way into it.

If we overemphasize things Canadian in our early reading, I think we may be forgiven for doing so. Until recently we have had to borrow most of our heroes from British and American writings. It is good for us to know that MacKenzie and Fraser and Thompson were heroes as well as Lewis and Clark, good to know that the law and order of the Northwest Mounted Police and our great early judges have a glory and meaning perhaps greater than that of the frontier marshal and the U.S. Cavalry. We are busy finding ourselves, and that is one of the ways of our young people into literature.

There is a librarian's saying – I am sure it must have been first said by a librarian – that "A boy may not be interested in books, but there are books about things a boy is interested in." The implication is that a child can be shown that books are useful, or that they can contribute to the pleasures he finds in other, usually more active, pursuits. Once he accepts this, there is always a reasonable hope that he may go a step further and realize that reading in itself can become a satisfying and lively interest.

This appeal to special interests is a perfectly legitimate one. One of the functions of books and reading is to supply information, and another is to supply pleasure through vicarious experience. Books on such matters as baseball and football, guns and hunting, skin-diving, skiing, hot rods, and fishing rods, belong in all young people's libraries and are read in Canada with the same interest as they are elsewhere. And Canadian girls in the country areas, and I suspect also in the cities, read "horse books"–horse books of every conceivable kind from the most intricately technical to the most outrageously fictional.

Reading that remains limited to these special interests is, however, little more than a pacifier–it keeps children quiet, gives them something to do, lets them fill out little cards to satisfy teachers. It does not of itself lead into that massive accumulation of human thought and feeling and experience that is literature.

There have always been good natural readers–children or sometimes older people–who turn to books with omnivorous delight from the first opportunity. These may present some special challenges for librarians, but no real problems. Many children are directed towards good reading by family influence and example. A librarian's problem here is simply that of keeping up with the child, of detecting the standards that have been reached and advancing them when possible. But the art of reading does not come naturally or by family example to *enough* children to ensure that under our systems–Canadian and American–constructive and intelligent people go out into society in sufficient quantity to protect and maintain human progress. Social democracy, which we both prefer and practise, holds the illusion that every man's opinion is as good as the next. This is a pathetic weakness, and it can be countered only by creating a higher proportion of people whose opinions really are worth something. Librarians have an important part to play in this.

I am thinking now of librarians as not merely keepers of books, but knowers of books and lovers of books. Reading and knowing books, I suspect, is the first duty of librarians. Only after that are the classification systems and the mechanics of library-keeping important. A librarian in his library is an authority–on books. He will be consulted and his opinions will be valued. For many there is no other way into the essential world of books than through the librarian.

If I were a children's librarian I think my first and greatest care would be the teachers of children. We have in Canada, as I am sure you have in the United States, great numbers of uneducated teachers—non-reading teachers, that is, for the two are indissolubly inseparable; the failure of method without broad knowledge is absolute. But most teachers are on the edge of being readers. A good high-school librarian can, by understanding the needs of teachers, by studying their interests and inclinations, and above all by *knowing* books and literature, do more for children's reading through service to teachers than in any other way. If teachers are readers, the children who have it in them to read at all will come to them more than half prepared for what they have to offer.

Here let me digress for a moment to a sharply practical consideration. In our country—perhaps also in the United States—books are not considered the tools of a teacher's trade. A government, theoretically composed of thinking men, does not consider teachers' nor, I suspect, librarians' book purchases as legitimate income-tax deductions. Whether teachers and librarians have made representations about this, I do not know. If they have not, they should. Every book and periodical a teacher buys, every book and periodical a librarian buys, is inevitably a tool of his trade. Furthermore, teachers and librarians would not have to make representations about anything so self-evident as this were it not that non-reading people elect legislators who do not understand the importance of reading.

I see the librarian as a dispenser of books, someone concerned not with how many books are on the shelves, but how many can be kept in circulation. Of course there are budgets to be considered and losses to be accounted for and a mass of administrative details to be attended to that have little to do with books as books. But I do not see the librarian as a cold servant of files and catalogues, I see him as the sympathetic

85

friend of all who come to the library, knowing that books are for people and unread books are of little value. If this is an erroneous picture, please do not disillusion me. This may be a writer's view, but I think that the ideal fate for a library book is to become worn out and replaced. If it is lost before it is worn out, that is sad; but it is far better lost and loved than left on the shelves.

Only good writing can suggest and reveal the power of good literature – reason enough in itself for librarians to know the difference between good and bad writing and to know which books on their shelves are well written and which badly written.

For young children, and for most older children, the power of good writing is most readily revealed in narrative. A good story encloses and enfolds a child, takes him up with it, creates a world for him and gives him memories. That is why Canadian children read the Hornblower stories of C.S. Forester, which are not Canadian stories at all, and the Jalna stories of Mazo de la Roche, which are Canadian, and J.B. Lippincott's animal stories, which are American – good stories, of whatever nationality, well told in good language.

Young children also like stories with which they can readily identify themselves. That is why boys like stories of both world wars, preferably of the forces of their own nation and preferably true – an official war history, even though officially dull in spots, may be read to tatters. Little girls like what my daughter calls "girl" stories – stories of somewhat older girls, perhaps Canadian, perhaps American, perhaps English. As I remember it, distantly over the years, when a small boy at school, one eagerly read stories about larger boys in larger schools. It seems natural enough to be inevitable, and while the majority of such stories may not be of the highest order, they fill a need of some sort and probably play their part in creating an interest in reading for the sake of reading.

It is important not to forget the power of narrative poems. Good modern narrative poems that appeal readily to children are scarce, and fashion tends away from the great Victorians. Fashion of this sort is readily imposed upon children – their elders and betters simply hide the poets and their work away from them. I believe this is a serious mistake. The narrative poems of people like Scott, Tennyson, and Kipling are supremely good work and can have immense appeal. They are also readily recognizable as good work, as precise literary form that powerfully and exactly achieves its purpose. Once read, they become valued memories and almost inevitably lead into the search for further experience. Nor would I have you forget such poets as Oliver Goldsmith and Thomas Love Peacock. Among the moderns, Stephen Vincent Benét and Edna St. Vincent Millay come readily to mind. The reach from good narrative verse into the finest poetry is not really very far, and a child who has found his satisfactions in narrative is ready to make it.

I could pursue this matter further and tell you that the product of modern education lacks an educated frame of reference, but I am sure you have heard it all before. The child or adult who lacks all knowledge of Greek and Roman literature comes to most modern literature at a grave disadvantage. Perhaps the answer to this is in the modern translations of the classics, and especially in the work of Robert Graves; but a suggestion such as this is in the nature of repairs for adults rather than opportunity for children. I can only urge upon you the importance of encouraging any sign of interest in Greek and Roman civilization.

I have so far been neglecting books written especially for children. This is at least partly because I believe that children were never better served in this way than they are today. Never before have there been children's books in such variety and quantity, so well written, planned, produced, and illustrated. A librarian's difficulty must be to find the ideal ways among all this excellence. I can suggest only a few guiding rules. In the first place, avoid all simplifications, abridgments, and rewrites. They do not belong on library shelves or anywhere else that I know of. Try, if you can, to keep away from those long series of books written around a single character or shell of a character. You can't avoid them – they fill a need, I know, and even the most alert of children is likely to find a way into them and drug himself with a quick surfeit. For many children they become an addiction as deadly as marijuana and may provide years of insulation from anything that could really be called reading.

It is important to look for good, simple style, sharp characterization, and concrete situations, all of which are made to carry ideas naturally and effectively. These are the modern standards of children's writing, and there is no need to bother much with books that do not come up to them.

Non-fiction books probably maintain even higher standards, on the average, than fiction. I do not profess to know my way around them as I am sure you do, but in the United States you have a series of historical biography called the "Landmark Series"; we in Canada have a rough equivalent, narrower in scope and directed, I think, to rather older children, called "Great Stories of Canada." Our children read your "Landmark Series" and I hope there is also a place in your libraries for our series. We all benefit by exchanges of this sort.

Books of these types lead readily into more advanced reading, and librarians should be very quick to serve any sign of such awakening interest. The straightforward biography of an early explorer may lead to curiosity about his contemporaries, the native peoples he met with, the particular country he traversed, the events that followed his discoveries. A library should be ready to provide further reading on these and similar points, and a librarian should be alert to suggest alternative sources when his own are exhausted. As a simple example of this type of progressive reading, I should like to tell of a Grade Eleven student in a rural western high school. This Canadian boy happened on an account of Confederate generals in an encyclopedia. He knew little or nothing of the Civil War, and very little more of American history in general, but the southern generals interested him and he read in quick succession such books as *Reveille in Washington, This Hallowed Ground, The Crisis, The Epic of America, Little Shepherd of Kingdom Come*, and *John Brown's Body*. He may or may not become one more dedicated student of the American Civil War – I rather hope he will not. But he had learned a lot about reading and the power of libraries in a very short while, and there is an excellent chance that he will apply it to many other subjects.

The move from children's reading into adult reading should never be delayed or held back. Naturally a librarian is sometimes afraid that a child may be discouraged by a book that is "too old" or "too difficult." It is a fair comment to suggest this – doing so sets up a challenge that is more than likely to be accepted – but it is wrong to insist on it. I will venture the proposition that an adult book, which holds a child's interest, is always better for him than a child's book. There may be exceptions to this, but they are not many and are not likely to be found in libraries designed primarily for children.

Censorship by exclusion is, I suppose, part of a librarian's duties. But I suggest to you that the censorship should always be on literary rather than on moral grounds. Any educated person – I am choosing my words with care – knows or has ready means of knowing that *The Catcher in the Rye* is a good book, seriously and purposefully written by an able writer, and therefore an effective and valuable means of adding growth and interest to a child's mind. I think it is immensely to the credit of librarians that they have stood firmly against the literary ignorance of educators and administrators and declared themselves on these points.

A declaration for a book on literary grounds is always a declaration on safe grounds – it may not always protect jobs, but it protects integrity and it is easily supported. And in this particular case there is also the justification of the special interest – almost the special claim of children on the book's contents.

No doubt some of you are wondering about other books of high literary quality and doubtful content. I can tell you a little story about at least one of them. Last fall, I was autographing books in a store when the librarian of a private school brought several of the older boys down to see me. They were politely interested in this healthy assignment, though rather less so than was the librarian. Three or four of them slipped away while her attention was still engaged and quickly purchased copies of *Lady Chatterley's Lover*. I admit this delighted me and I am sure they got a lot of added pleasure from their well-conducted enterprise. But I wonder if it was any better for them to get the book in this way than with the full consent of authority. They are going to read it because it is now a part of English literature and it is entirely unlikely that they can be harmed by it; but the illicit acquisition no doubt raises hopes of harm which should not be there and so risks making a disappointment out of what should have been a fine literary experience.

Canadian children read much like children anywhere. They are interested in stories about their own country, in stories of adventure, travel, and the frontier. They also read books like *Anne of Green Gables* and *The Secret Garden* and *Treasure Island* because the authors of these books have a special way into the desires of a child's heart. They turn readily to a book like *The Diary of Anne Frank* if their attention is directed to it – not merely because it has a special contemporary interest, but because it is a touching human document. My twelve-year-old daughter had read Joy Adamson's *Born Free* within three hours of its arrival in the house. Children read books like Hugh McLennan's *Barometer Rising*, and no doubt go on in time to other works by this fine Canadian novelist.

Canadian children also read many books that are not much good for anything, but I doubt if they are greatly harmed by doing so. Inferior standards of thinking and writing do not entertain a competent mind for very long – it reaches out for better things. One of the most important duties of a librarian is to make sure that better things are always within reach. Good reading is a constant search – for entertainment and excitement, for knowledge and understanding and ideas. The librarian is the guardian and guide on this search, and in large measure the protector of its standards. Librarians are undoubtedly the most powerful single influence in book publishing today, and children's librarians can well take much of the credit for the present high standards of children's books. I am not sure what rewards children's librarians ask of their work – perhaps more good children's books to keep the customers happy. But the greatest reward must always be in watching the first stirrings of true intellectual curiosity, in giving guidance and stimulation to keep that curiosity alive and growing, and in seeing it reach out at last into the world of adult books.

Whether or not this is a reward, it is a service of supreme importance. Without good reading, human growth is slow at best. Without human growth, no civilization can long survive.

10

If Armageddon's On

(1939)

I had not supposed that the old reserve commission would ever catch up with me, yet that is exactly what it has done. In a few weeks now I shall be a second lieutenant starting on a six-thousand-mile journey to help fight a war. It is twelve or thirteen years since I went on the reserve and in that time I have grown so far away from what I was that the thing seems to have no connection with me. Yet here I am waiting to be called up, almost afraid they may have forgotten me or do not want me, knowing perfectly well that if the certainty of being called did not exist I should be looking for some other way of getting into trouble. A habit of articulateness, developed by years of putting things down on paper, makes it essential that I account for what seems a renunciation of most of the ideas I have held through my adult life.

I am, after all, about as happily and comfortably situated as any man could ask to be. I am thirty-one, which is young enough for a vigorous strength of mind and body and old enough for fairly intelligent direction of both. I have been married for nearly six years to a red-haired American girl, who fills every ideal I have ever had of what a wife and a woman should be. I have two small daughters, brown little creatures with brown hair bleached to a pale blonde by this summer's sun. I own a pleasant house in British Columbia, set in twenty acres of land on the banks of a fine river. I like books and have a library of fifteen hundred volumes that holds more good matter than many I have seen of ten times the size. I like fly fishing, and there is plenty of it within easy reach of me. I like wing shooting and can find enough of it to get good work out of my Labradors every year. Finally, I am reasonably successful in my profession of writing, which I prefer to all others, and I like my future prospects very well.

That I am willing to risk all this for the chance of standing room in a trench surprises me. Yet in spite of intellectual reservations and a normal reluctance, I am willing. Training and family background, which led up to that reserve commission, have something to do with it – though a good deal less, I honestly believe, than might be expected. I was born into an English family, whose every other male member was in some sort of peace-time soldiering before 1914. I was sent to one of the larger and more famous public schools and was expected to go from there to the army or one of the civil services, probably by way of Oxford or Cambridge. On the face of it, that should have made me a pushover for the recruiting officer in any of the Empire's wars.

But I do not think I was ever really in tune with what was planned for me. I found school rules a list of provocations, and the picturesque method of enforcing them with stick or birch was simply a challenge. I felt then, and I still believe I was right, that if one were skilful enough to avoid the punishments, or tough enough to be prepared to endure them, one was entitled to break rules. The authorities, of course, had one more idea than I had and they expelled me in the end, judging that I was not amenable to discipline – and under that particular set-up I certainly was not, though I have not been in much trouble since I got away from it. Oxford and Cambridge warned me that they would deal in the same way with the first mistake I chose to make and I preferred not to chance it. A very brief taste of peace-time soldiering persuaded me that the job did not offer what I was looking for and I left that – with my reserve commission.

I think that is fair enough evidence that I am essentially resistant to the training that has always made empire-builders and empire-defenders of the approved type. The logging camps of Washington and British Columbia completed the weaning from any tendency I may have had to behave as my family expected me to, and my training sought to ensure that I would. In the late twenties, there was a fine spirit of independence in those camps; if you didn't like the colour of your foreman's shirts you could tell him to go to hell and look for another man as good as you; it was never hard to find another job with a foreman who had better taste in shirts.

Working in the logging camps I became confirmed in an intention I had always had to write. A kind editor published something for me when I was fourteen years old and so convinced me that I should come to the profession sooner or later, even though by way of the civil service or the army. In the camps, writing and thinking about writing, provided me with a much needed mental outlet. My first book was published in 1931, and I have called myself a writer ever since. I like the practice of the profession as well as I had liked the idea of it and I have always taken the job seriously – perhaps too seriously for my own financial good. But now, after four books and ten years of self-training, I feel that I am ready to produce what I have always wanted to – good solid fiction about human beings. The way to this has been through the things I knew and felt fitted to handle – birds, fish, animals, and the open country of British Columbia. My upbringing did at least make me a good fly fisherman, a keen and accurate observer, and an admirer of decent writing. If I have broken away far enough to find a sympathetic understanding of people, I have also followed the original direction to the point of becoming a tolerably good amateur biologist.

I suppose no young Canadian or American writer, starting to learn his job in the thirties, could possibly avoid getting a good shot of radicalism. I was resistant for a while – training and family background again – but now my conservative friends call me a good scarlet radical. My radical friends call me a good solid conservative. That puts me in a pleasant no-man's land whence I can take occasional shots at both sides. Applying the point directly to the people I want to write about – the loggers and other working men of British Columbia – I find myself loathing bitterly the blacklist system, the discrimination against married men, the suppression of union activity, the absentee ownership of operations, which threatens future timber supplies and destroys any chance of proper sympathy and understanding between owners and men, and the speed-up system that has killed so many of my friends. At the same time, I can find it in me to be afraid of excessive union domination, to admire the passionate individuality of the loggers, deplore their tendency to contribute to the speed-up, and despise the too often distorted pictures of the labour agitators as likely to fail in their objective. In other words, though I am pro-labour, and would jump to the bright side of the barricades as soon as they were erected, I think I can claim to have a tolerably open mind.

This progressive defection from the way of life into which I was born brought me at one point within measurable distance of calling myself a pacifist. But I couldn't quite manage it; the effectiveness of pacifism has always seemed to me dependent upon the other fellow holding fast to the same attitude or at least starting out with some pretty definite scruples about attacking the defenceless and undefending, and in my short lifetime it has never seemed that mankind was in just the right frame of mind to make such universal forbearance probable. Without belief in the fairly immediate effectiveness of pacifism, I could not possibly find the courage to face what being a conscientious objector would mean, so I have never played with that idea. But I have devoutly believed, almost up to the present time, that no nation which suffered at all deeply during the last war would ever permit its government

95

to fight again except as a last resort against attack. And that seemed to place war – that is war that would affect me directly – as a pretty remote possibility.

What we are already learning to call the First Great War killed my father and three of my uncles. For six months after my father's death in 1918, I hated the enemy with all the black bitterness that a ten-year-old could summon. But it was not too hard, even for a ten-year-old, to realize after a little while the impersonal nature of the killing. I still regret my father's death, because what I knew of him and what I have been able to find out about him seems strong and good. Though he had published three books and some hundreds of thousands of words in periodicals before the war, he was what I believe is known as a "late developer." He was killed as a colonel in March 1918, when he was forty years old, and a late developer with three and a half years of war inside him might have been able to stir something big. Certainly he had a strong and simple prose style and a sound knowledge of verse forms that would have enabled him to say big things clearly.

My three uncles who died, a doctor, a barrister, and a professional soldier, were probably the most aggressive and brilliant men among my mother's eleven brothers. So I am able to judge the cost of war pretty accurately from my immediate personal experience. I have been able to tell myself ever since the First Great War that a Second Great War would make those deaths sheer waste. For that reason I have resisted, in my puny way, any government that showed signs of considering a Second Great War as a possibility. I have favoured disarmament and friendship with former enemy countries. I have despised nationalism, loathed patriotism, and even learned to doubt my country's motives in the First Great War. But this last year has shifted my conception of mankind and its degree of civilization. I no longer feel that those deaths may have been wasted. They bought for me twenty years of peace, freedom, and good life; and that, multiplied as it must be by many millions, is a lot.

But this need not force me back upon an intense patriotism and a narrow nationalism. I have never felt a considered hate against any nation and I cannot feel any now. I cannot even find it in me, as some more gentle people can, to hate Herr Hitler. He seems a sad, sincere, courageous, John Citizen man, pathetically ignorant and perhaps pathetically conceited. For nearly two years he has seemed diabolically clever, a superb opportunist, but now he has betrayed even that idea of him. That he genuinely believes he is serving the best interests of his nation, and perhaps also (though by no means necessarily) of the people of his nation, I still have no doubt – though I suspect the slope is steeper than he thought it was and perhaps now he would like a different wax on his skis. I find I have not lost an intense desire, conceived during the Munich crisis, to know enough of the man and his life to be able to write a five-hundred-page novel about him. I should not expect to find, even in that full knowledge, anything to make me hate him.

Having no hate, and having nothing concrete to gain, I must have other reasons for going voluntarily to war. Atrocities do not stir me: I do not believe in them. I believe, for instance, that the bombing of civilian populations is an inevitable by-product of the bombing of military objectives. During the First Great War, I saw the effect of a bomb that had fallen on a house which stood right beside a children's hospital in Chelsea; the nearest military objective was Victoria Station, fully a mile away; yet I have little doubt that Victoria Station was what the man at the release lever hoped to hit. In any case, I question whether it is as essentially wicked to kill old people and children as it is to kill young men in the prime of their strength and usefulness; whether it is as essentially wicked to kill crippled and wounded under a red cross as it is to kill the strong and healthy out in the open. That this is an intellectual rather than an emotional conviction I am prepared to admit, since I should not myself be willing to attempt to kill old women and wounded men, though I am apparently willing to attempt to kill the young and well and strong. But a hundred Athenias and a thousand Llandovery Castles could not make me thirst for revenge against men only indirectly connected with such happenings.

Not hate. Not indignation. Standard of living perhaps? I think so, and in this is the root of all wars. We have been shown that in democratic countries it is still true that the people, not their governments, make wars. True also that in making them the people are defending the interests of the capitalists. But in a capitalist country the interests of the workers and the capitalists cannot be sharply separated; even when capital is state-owned it is the same – power and prosperity for capital means power and prosperity for the worker: high wages, high standard of living. The workers of Canada, the United States, and Great Britain have a comparatively high standard of living and though they would not be willing to fight other nations to impove that standard, I suspect they will always fight to maintain it. I question whether this is a defensible attitude, though I defend it to myself by saying: "Don't drag us down to your level. Come up to ours. We'll help you – if we can, without going down." It is a bitter, unfriendly defence, akin to that of a millionaire arguing with a communist, and some day it may be forgotten. When it is the nations will be at peace. In the meanwhile, I have little doubt that any nation seeking world domination is threatening the standard of living in my own country – and I know enough of conditions in my own country to feel that this is a stirring threat.

More immediately and personally, I want the right to live and work in my own way, without interference from crises and alarms. In the last two years the threat of war has become so insistent that peaceful and useful work of all kinds, in all countries, has been thrust steadily farther and farther into the background. Since 1935, I have been making a new book; I do not pretend that it is a tremendously significant book, but

I know it fills a constructive and useful purpose, and it is unquestionably of importance to me and to my family. During the writing of it war came very close – not once, but half a dozen times – and I had to face the fact that the book might be rendered valueless before it was finished. I finished it two or three months after the Munich crisis; a few days before Britain and France declared war I corrected the last of the American galleys. Probably there will not be an English edition now. I can accept the fact that my book is a small thing and I am a small thing in the world. But I am bigger sitting at my desk and writing my book than I can possibly be in a trench; and there are tens of millions of others who are bigger if left undisturbed to their own work than they can ever be masquerading as soldiers or running from air raids. We have tried to work on the idea that peace can come without war from a long series of crises and alarms. It has been made sufficiently evident that it cannot, and it now seems better to become little for a short, intense period than to be whittled smaller and smaller through years of dragging interruptions, only to have to face the horror in the end.

"National honour" is a phrase that does not stack up well against a threat to the lives and happiness of millions of people; it seems at first merely an abstraction compounded of aggressive pride and patriotism. But it may also mean a willingness to come to agreements and abide by them, to make promises and keep them, to state a policy and hold to it honestly; and in those things is the only hope of secure peace in a world whose international relationships are anarchic. That seems to be in the song that the foreign correspondents have sung for us. Until Munich, I believed that any avoidance of war was good and honourable, not shameful. The by-line boys have been at great pains to change all that – and after all, why not? As my favourite baseball announcer is always saying when the fans get excited: "There's no extra charge for umpiring the game from behind the net." But what they have been saying since Munich has been hard to take, even though the country they love best to fret at had made no promise to fight for "poor little Czechoslovakia." Having taken all that, swallowed it down without too wry a face, perhaps it is not too soon to be ready to defend "national honour." After all, Poland had and needed a promise.

These reasons are all somewhat negative – I suppose a man's reasons for going to a defensive war must be negative. Negative and defensive as they are they would probably be enough to persuade me to go voluntarily, if bitterly. But I can find also positive reasons, reasons that stem from my life, from where I live and from what I hope to do. The men I go with will be Canadians, most of them from British Columbia. They will be miners, loggers, fishermen, farmers, longshoremen, storekeepers, the men I write about and about whom I want to write more. They are the livest and best part of British Columbia and their going will be the livest thing that happens to the province until they return. It will touch and pattern and mark everything that happens in the years after they get back; to know what will be in them then I must have known whatever it is they go to.

I am in the middle of them in time as well as place. The youngest of them will be eighteen, the oldest forty-five. I am thirty-one. Going with them and being of them I may be able to help at times; there is more to a war than just fighting and men, particularly young men and simple men, need more than food and boots and ammunition.

War, for an infantry soldier, is likely to be generally uncomfortable, frequently terrifying, and sometimes dangerous. From six thousand miles and perhaps several months away one cannot properly appreciate the danger. The possibility of getting killed is a gloomy one – there is so much to come back to, there are so many things one would like to see and feel and do again, so many things yet unseen and unfelt and untouched. I know that I have accepted the possibility because I have told my wife things that would not

100

otherwise have been important, and because I feel an insistent drive to commit as much of my mind as I can to paper. This drive is stronger than the more obvious things; I should like to take my fly rod and go up the river again, to take my dogs and find some grouse again – the season opened today; but there doesn't seem to be time for those things, greatly as I have loved them. I want to get this down and pass on to the next thing and the next. It is a primitive urge to a highly civilized action; clearly it is closely akin to the urge that sends young men and women hurrying off to buy marriage licences and reproduce themselves as soon as they are threatened by war. I want to leave as much as possible behind me, to separate from myself as much of myself as I can, so that if I must die and rot there will be less to rot with me. I want to keep on writing all through the time of being away, partly for this same reason and partly because the habit is precious; it would not be good to let years go by without writing.

The prospect of being scared and uncomfortable is more real and in many ways more serious than the possibility of being killed. It seems somehow important to try and remain objective about the war itself, though without denying oneself a feather's weight of sympathetic feeling for the men who will be fighting it. From close and honest observation of this sort it should be possible to learn something; but discomfort and fear are powerful enemies of objectivity.

Whatever luck I may have, many men, many good men, will be killed – many have been killed already. It is hard to see what will grow out of their deaths or what their deaths will mean – harder this time than last, because we know more and have seen more. Perhaps there will be another twenty years of peace and social progress for the nations that bred them up to die in war. Perhaps there will be a longer peace than just twenty years. If one could know it would be easier to judge what purpose war serves; it might be possible to work the thing out in figures, as a biologist should, balancing survivals against losses, misery and stagnation against happiness and

101

growth. I can find the faint lines of a pattern in it. The death of my father and millions like him gave twenty years of peace to me and tens of millions like me. If we die now, in our millions, must our sons die too in their millions, twenty years from now? The thing is too faint to read clearly, the figures and samples and tests are too few and too incomplete to yield sound conclusions. But in my own case, at least, the progression seems against the possibility. My father died at forty and left a ten-year-old son. I am a little over thirty and shall die, if I die, when my elder child is three or four. Perhaps some wise man will make something of that and persuade the world to grant another generation the right to die of old age.

11
The Bells
(1950)

At the time of V-E Day, Ken and I were stuck in administrative jobs at a hospital near the border of Hampshire and Surrey. Word came through promptly that no Canadian troops from outside London would be allowed to go up there for the celebrations on May 8. Ken, a schoolteacher from Toronto, very earnest about his discovery of England and the whole island story, was disgusted.

"Here we are," he said, "within fifty miles of the very heart of everything, at the biggest moment in all history. And they won't even let us take a look at it."

"Wild Canadians," I said. "Likely we'd get drunk and bust up the show. I think maybe they've got something."

I realized I didn't want to go, anyway. Everybody in London would be on the streets, yelling and getting tight, and we'd see nothing for the crowds. "Listen, Ken," I said. "If you want to tell your grandchildren you saw England on V-E Day, I know the way to go about it."

"How?"

"Winchester. That was the capital of England long before London. Winchester Cathedral is more history than Westminster Abbey will ever be. Roman England, Saxon England, Norman England—you can find all of them right around Winchester," I said.

Ken nodded. "You could be right, at that. How'll we get there?"

"Bikes," I told him. "There's a couple of orderlies will rent them. That way, you can see rural England celebrating, too."

That was on May 7. We started out early the next morning and at once ran into two gigantic hills. It was over thirty miles to Winchester and I have never been an enthusiastic cyclist, but soon we hit some good going and made time. In the villages, flags were out and people were placidly getting ready to hear Churchill's speech on the radio at three o'clock. Twice we were stopped by happy but subdued groups of elderly farmers and other countrymen, who were determined to distribute free beer from open casks outside small pubs.

After the second stop, Ken said, "They sure are a quiet people. What makes you think there'll be anything more happening at Winchester."

"Bound to be," I said. "That cathedral is important to England. They have to do something there. All we have to do is be there by three o'clock."

We were near Alton. I glanced up at a fine tree by the side of the road, saw a tablet, and read that the tree had been planted by Jane Austen. I showed it to Ken and he was impressed, but I could see that his mind was still in London. I wondered about Winchester, whether we should find what he wanted there. At least he could see the school, and all schools interested him. I had previously shown him Charterhouse, in Surrey, where I had once gone to school, and given him such inside knowledge of the place as I had. And over beyond Winchester there was Twyford, which I had attended for three years before going to Charterhouse. But schools seemed hardly enough for this day. Ken had to have something from England that would set this day apart from all the other days of his life.

104

We were still making good time, and as we came into the Itchen valley, I stopped at a brick bridge over a small tributary. It was a perfect chalkstream, quick-flowing over clean gravel. All the chalkstream creatures were moving within sight: moor hens and wagtails, a water ouzel, a hatch of blue-winged olives floating down the surface, and two fine trout rising to them just above the bridge. I pointed all this out to Ken but knew it did not touch him.

"How come you know so much about Hampshire?" he asked as we rode on.

"I've fished it. It's a good fishing county," I said. "I've read about it, too. And I told you I was at school at Twyford. Then I was tutored for a year in history just this side of Winchester." I thought of David Gordon, the quiet, scholarly rector of a tiny parish who had guided me through Stubbs' Charters, Macaulay, and Trevelyan, with side glances at George Meredith and Jane Austen; Dav with his little Saxon church, his rock-solid Protestantism, his sense of history and of England. He would know something of what was going on in Winchester.

I had begun to recognize the country now, and because we were well ahead of time we decided to stop for lunch at Itchen Abbas. It was an unusually good lunch – fresh bread, plenty of cheese, lettuce, and hothouse tomatoes, and excellent beer. I could see Ken was feeling better.

"Well," he said, "what do we do now?"

"No use getting to Winchester much before Churchill speaks at three o'clock," I said. "That's over two hours yet. We'd better go in and see my old tutor. It's right on the road." We had another pint of beer, and I tried to tell him about Dav, who was not only scholar, but theologian, historian, sociologist; who farmed the parish glebe, sawed his own wood, and preached a fine sermon every Sunday; who stood so stoutly for the rights of Church against State in things both temporal and spiritual, yet never failed to follow and understand the changes of a changing world. "It's an important part of England," I said. "Something you must see to have seen this country at all. There's honest Saxon in the church and the main part of it is Norman. Cromwell's people did their usual job of breaking up some of the best stonework, but that's history, too. And the parish has everything – glebe and tithe and Queen Anne's Bounty. I forget most of it, but Dav will tell you."

We cycled along the road into a small village, and in almost no time had come to the rectory. I felt a sudden doubt. "Let's go on and look at the church," I said. "We can go in here later."

The church seemed exactly as I had last seen it, grey and square-towered, set in a quiet green graveyard by the swampy stream. It looked empty and ageless. I had been away from it only twenty years, but Dav I thought was mortal man, no longer young for all the cheerful strength I remembered in him. I had not heard of him for several years. He would not be as I had known him; he might even have died or gone away. When we got back to the rectory I was half afraid to go in. If Ken hadn't been there and I hadn't made the promise to him, I don't think I should have.

A country girl opened the door and I asked her if the Doctor was in. "He's upstairs resting," she said. "I'll ask if he will see you." She showed us into the study and I knew from a single glance at the books that it was still Dav's house. He came downstairs in four or five minutes, a little stooped, a little slower after two decades, but still the same black-coated man with the white string tie in place of the parson's dog collar. "Yes?" he asked courteously. "Yes? What can I do for you?"

I knew that the girl would have told him "two Canadians," though I had given her our names. I spoke mine to him, then repeated it as he peered at me. Suddenly, there was recognition in his eyes. "Why, Rod," he said. "Rod!"

So we sat in the study and talked of things twenty years

106

before. I tried to keep Dav to his church and parish as much as possible, for Ken's benefit.

"It has been a long, hard time," he said. "You would think this quiet little parish might have escaped most of it. But we've had our share of the bombing."

I thought of the simple, scattered houses of the village and asked him how it could have happened. "Luck," Dav said. "I suppose you'd call it that. Quite early, there was a direct hit on a row of cottages. Then the V-1s seemed to find us especially. Quite a lot of them fell near here and there were three hits. Perhaps that doesn't sound much to you, but it meant losses in nearly every family in the village, apart from those at the front."

"You look tired," I said. "No wonder."

Dav smiled. "We have had seventy-five evacuated children here ever since 1940. And the panic from Southampton was hard on us, too – they came all the way up here." Using his thumb, he tamped tobacco into his pipe, then shifted his spectacles up onto his forehead in a gesture I remembered.

The time had slipped by and it was almost three o'clock. He tuned in his radio, so we'd be ready to hear Churchill, and then, while we waited, he sat silent in his chair, his head bowed slightly as though the weight of the war years was far too much to shake away even in the moment of victory. It seemed unlike him. I thought to ask him what we should look for in Winchester later that afternoon, but changed my mind.

"Dav," I said, "something's wrong. It's not like you to be depressed at a time like this."

He looked up and smiled sadly. "I've got a burden," he said. "I was thinking of my bells. They've been rung for every great British victory since – well, since Agincourt. I'd like to say since Crécy and Poitiers, but I'm not sure they're quite so old as that. Today there's no one to ring them."

"You mean your ringers are all away in the services?"

"There isn't an able-bodied man left in the village."

"You just want a noise out of them, and there's no one even for that?" I glanced across at Ken and saw his eyes were bright with interest. I knew he was thinking, even as I was, of all those mighty names: Agincourt, Flodden Field, perhaps, and the Armada. Blenheim, Ramillies, Oudenarde, Malplaquet, Trafalgar, and Waterloo.

"I've got one man," Dav was saying. "He's not very strong, though. And three of the women have promised to come, if I want them. But the bells are heavy. I don't think they could make them sound."

"What about us?" I asked. "Ken and I. We've got weight enough."

Dav looked up again quickly. "Would you do that? Would you?"

"It'd be the proudest thing we ever did," I said.

Then Churchill came on, and Dav sat listening solemnly to the releasing words of the enormous day. As soon as it was over, he got his hat and cane, and the three of us walked slowly down to the church. Dav's lone man was already there. While Dav looked on, Ken and I each took a rope and the other man the third. I pulled mine, felt the bell swing, but there was no sound. We all three pulled our ropes, and still there was no sound. I remembered having seen bell-ringers at work, one foot in the sling below the tufted handhold: pull, release, stop with the foot, pull again. I tried it and my bell tolled once, then a second time. I signalled Ken and the other man, and they understood. First one bell, then the other, joined mine. I listened, trying to catch some rhythm or sequence we could control and repeat. But the bells took their own way with us, now singly, now in scaled sequence, now together in a clashing peal. After five minutes we began to sweat. Fifteen minutes Dav had said, and then was gone into the vestry. We gave him thirty, for the biggest and most dangerous of all victories.

The lone parishioner left us, and Ken and I went into the

108

vestry and found Dav kneeling there silently. The parish register was open in front of him, and he had entered the ringing of the bells and the date. Ken and I signed, adding rank and the habitual "Cdn. Army O/seas."

"Dav," I asked when he stood up, "how do you know the bells rang for Agincourt?"

"There's a record of it in the cathedral archives," he said. "And the phrasing suggests that wasn't the first time. But I've never been able to find out any more."

"Don't bells always have dates cast on them?"

"Not always, especially the early ones. We looked at these many years ago and there didn't seem to be any date."

"I'd like to look now," I said. "It would be good to know for sure."

"It's years since anyone went up. I'm afraid the ladders and staging may be rotten. Be careful."

Ken and I climbed into the tower among a maze of bleached, worm-eaten oak beams and braces, testing footholds, loosening dust, and breaking cobwebs. Some daylight came through the louvers of the tower, but it was difficult to see much. We struck several matches before we were satisfied that the surfaces of the two smaller bells were blank. The largest bell was hung well out from the staging, and its position as well as its bulk made it harder to check. The side nearest us had nothing. I got a foothold on a brace, leaned over, and managed to get my right hand against the cross-timber holding the bell. It had been a fairly athletic performance so far, but now I discovered a ledge close against the wall of the tower and reached it with my left foot. Straddled between this and the brace, I lit another match and found the inscription almost at once, on the far side of the bell. "*SANCTI*," the gothic letters said. "*1101 A.D.*" I read it out to Ken.

"Gosh," he said, and was silent.

"It's long past three o'clock," I said. "Do you want to go on to Winchester?"

He shook his head. "Not after this." He had scrambled

109

over near me, and I lit another match while he examined the date. He stared at it for what seemed a long time.

"Crécy, hell! These bells brought Coeur de Lion home from the Crusades," he said jubilantly.

Then the match went out and we climbed down.

12

Place des Cygnes

(1956)

My son Alan and I made a circle of the potholes on the last
day of duck season. It was a windless day, almost mild,
though there was snow on the northern slopes of the ridges
and every lake and pond for miles around had been frozen
for weeks past. We were at low elevation in logged-over
country, but even here there was open water only because
the short, deep ravines of this little section were fed by
underground seepage from the big lakes, too warm to freeze
in its brief run. Few of the beaver ponds were frozen and the
main stream, a good-sized creek of constant flow, was not
even iced along its edges.

Our search for ducks took us along a series of beaver
dams, winding towards the steep head of a draw to the north
of the main creek. We found only a few buffleheads, but the
likeliest place of all was still ahead. By swinging southward,
across two low ridges, we could come back to the main creek
where a well-placed beaver dam spread it into a dog-leg pool a
hundred yards long by thirty or forty wide. The sandy bottom
of the pool is weed-grown, even in winter, and its current is
broken by several great water-logged tree trunks; the swampy
edges grow strong grasses and weeds in black, peaty soil; if
there were any ducks that had not forsaken fresh water for

111

the tideflats, this was where they would be.

The pond is not an easy place to approach, especially on a windless day. We stopped at the crest of the second ridge to work out a plan. A hundred feet below us was a thicket of alders on a flat bench. Beyond them, I knew, the ground dropped away through another fifty feet or so to the edge of the pool. What little breeze there was came from downstream, so I decided to send Alan to wait at the bend below the dam while I made a wide circle to come out at the head of the pool. I had begun to explain the plan to him when a single, deep, musical *kronk* from beyond the alders made us both drop to our knees. "Geese," I whispered and my mind began to search furiously for some better way to approach them. But there were other sounds from the pool now, the splashings of heavy birds taking off from the water. They could not have seen us or winded us, and I felt they would not have heard us; the splashings were so heavy and so prolonged that I wondered if something else might have disturbed them—a deer starting ahead of us out of the alder thicket, perhaps even a cougar making an attack of his own on one of their number.

Then we saw the first flight; huge white birds in line on slow wings behind the bare tops of the alders, lifting steadily as they passed downstream, then swinging left to cross no more than fifty feet above the ridge we were crouched on. The sun was setting somewhere in the clouds behind us and there was a faint pink flush on the white feathers of the swans, repeated again on the distant white peaks of the mainland mountains just under their line of flight. There were six of them, two in line ahead, four others grouped in rough formation just behind the second; all were pure white adults, long-necked, great-bodied, with jet-black bills, jet-black legs, and feet held closely against their feathers. While they were still in sight, Alan's breathless whisper turned me to see the second flight, as it swung over the ridge to the west of us, no higher than the first and as close, so that the pattern of the feathers was visible on the white bodies and the sound of the sweeping wings was strong and clear.

We turned to each other, awed, yet laughing with joy at the tremendous thing we had seen and the way we had seen it. And it still was not over. A single swan, slow-winged and calm yet swifter in flight than the fastest duck or goose, came down the pool, lifted to the ridge, and passed right over our heads to join the others.

These were trumpeter swans, a scattering from the big band of a hundred or so that always winters somewhere in the valley, usually in the swamps at the head of the second big lake. But it was a much larger group than I had ever before seen away from the main band or in such a tiny pool. The temptation to go in there again was enormous, but I held off, for many reasons. The weather was bad, with frequent snowfalls and steady freezing, so I was fairly certain the birds would cling to the open creek. I did not want to disturb them too often and still less did I want to advertise their presence by beating a track in the snow that others might follow. But towards the end of February, I knew the time had come to look for them again. Within a few weeks, a month at most, they would leave the valley to travel north.

I chose a clear, sunny afternoon with a moderate, but steady, westerly breeze. There was snow on the ground, soft and rotten in the exposed places, but a foot deep in any sort of shade and on all the northern faces. Because the wind was westerly I decided to work up the creek, against it, towards the pool. I thought the swans would be feeding in the swampy edge on the crook of the dog-leg, and hoped I would be able to come close enough to get a good sight through glasses without disturbing them.

Cutting across the deep draws towards the creek – I had long ago decided never to go or come the same way twice – I wondered why I should believe they would still be there, in that tiny place, after a full month. There was the freezing weather, of course, but that was hardly enough; the big lakes

113

along the main flow of the watershed were nearly always open where the larger streams came into them and the swans had wintered there safely for hundreds of years. This winter was no worse than a dozen others I remembered, not nearly so bad as some of them. But it was the winter that meant the first stages of destruction for the swans' old wintering grounds.

Ever since fall, men and machines had been moving in to clear the edges of the two upper lakes and build the dam that would flood them. There was a big camp at the edge of the great swamp on the second lake, the favourite wintering place of them all; logging machines clattered on the sides of the sloughs, cables slapped at the brush and tore away the trees that had been cut down. For the most part, the birds had accepted this calmly enough; after all, the open water, the grasses and seeds and roots they needed were still there and would be until the water came up behind the dam. But my birds, I felt sure, had not accepted it. They had been driven to the tiny beaver pond by the disturbance rather than by the freezing weather.

I chose to go into the pond against the wind, because it was impossible to move silently, or even quickly, on the half-rotten snow. But this brought me also squarely against the sun and I came in sight of the deep bend of the pool before I really expected to. I was still well back from the steep bank that dropped down to the lower end of the pond, among a scattering of young alders about a hundred yards from the bend. I stopped sharply and strained my eyes for sight of the swans, but the slant of the sun and the scattered snow patches made everything uncertain, so I began to search the grass clumps in the bend through the glasses. I found them. At first two birds, close together, feeding; then another single one beyond them. The distance was too great to see them as I really wanted to and the alders spoiled even the distant view I had. They had not seen me, but I was more afraid of their hearing than of their sight. I dropped to my knees and began

114

to creep forward, cursing every rustle and crunch of the snow under my weight. I had covered perhaps thirty or forty feet when I heard the single warning *kronk* from somewhere much closer than the birds I was watching. I stopped and held my breath for as long as I could, but the warning note sounded again. Five swans came swimming upstream from under the high bank that still hid the tail of the pool from my sight.

Kneeling in the snow, I lifted the glasses carefully and focussed on them. The glare of sun from the water made a bad light, but the swimming birds were a noble picture. Their necks were straight and high, white bodies floated well up on the water, glistening wakes streamed out behind them as they made way easily against the current. They were obviously alert, but not afraid or particularly disturbed and I hoped they might move up with the other three and settle to feeding. But their warning and movement had alerted the whole pond. A group of mallards talked nervously on the far side. I caught the movement of other ducks here and there while I watched the splendid procession move on, around the end of the first big log, into open water beyond that would bring them up to the other swans.

Then the nervous mallards took flight, a dozen of them clattering steeply up against the wind, followed at intervals by smaller groups. The swans seemed to be swimming more swiftly away from me. Suddenly the great white wings were spread, powerful black feet paddled once or twice against the surface of the water, the wings themselves touched water twice, perhaps three times, and the five were away in clear flight, rising visibly on every wing thrust. I watched in admiration, expecting the other three to join them, but they did not, though the bugle notes of the flying birds seemed to call them. The two nearer ones had stopped their feeding and were standing straight among the tussocks of grass. The third, perhaps ten or fifteen yards beyond them, was floating in a little channel of water among the grass clumps, still feeding steadily. One of the nearer birds walked a few dignified steps and flapped its wings vigorously. The other walked towards it. Then, both were still except for little up and down movements of their heads and long, straight necks as they talked in short, soft musical sounds that barely reached me on the wind.

Again I hoped they would settle down. Again I was disappointed. Together they made two or three short, heavy steps, necks stretched forward, wings spread, and they were flying away into the wind after the others. But the lone bird made no move to follow.

I was afraid for it then, afraid it was sick or wounded. For a little while I watched as it fed, curving the long neck forward and down full length into the water, lifting it back to full straight stretch for a moment, plunging it down again. Then I began to move up. Soon I had to pass out of sight into the alder thicket. I worked through as quickly and silently as I could, but when I came in sight again the bird was swimming strongly up the middle of the pond, fifty or sixty yards away, turning its head and making soft, deep sounds that seemed nervous now that it was alone. I still supposed it must be hurt in some way, so I held on quite boldly and steadily towards it. It took off with the same astonishing ease as the others and flew after them.

As the swan passed out of sight around the curve of the high banks upstream, the pond seemed utterly desolate. I looked for ducks and saw only a single merganser towards the downstream end – but a tiny merganser, so small that I thought it couldn't be a merganser. I put the glasses on her and still couldn't believe what I saw. She was certainly a merganser and an American merganser at that, not even a redbreast. But a miniature bird; I felt puzzled, but really had no time for her.

The two swans that had flown together had swung back down the pool, passing within fifty or sixty yards of me, then turned away towards the north. But the first five and the last lone one had not reappeared and I felt they might have turned southward towards little Hidden Lake, which lay just over the ridge. The chance of another sight of them was too good to miss, so I crossed the creek and ploughed through the deep, soft snow of the north face until I topped the ridge and saw that Hidden Lake was solidly frozen. I turned back, coming to the creek again by the beaver dam at the downstream end of the long pool. The merganser was still there, the only bird on the pond. But she was a fine big bird now. Her russet head was bright, her pale breast smooth, the grey plumage of her wings and back shone in the sunlight. If anything, I thought, she was a little larger than normal size.

Ten days later I went into the pool again. This time I held well to the westward, aiming to come in from the upstream side. There was no wind and it was a dry, dull day; but it was much milder, and on the southerly slopes the snow lay only in scattered patches. I topped the last low ridge slowly and cautiously, keeping down and searching for clear, soft ground at every step. Again it seemed almost foolish to hope that the swans would still be there, but from the crest of the ridge I could see part of the grassy flat in the bend of the pool, through a screening of stumps and small trees. There was a small white patch, half-hidden by grass clumps. Even before I put up the glasses, I knew it was a swan.

The ground ahead sloped easily to a little bench that ran out to the steep bank just above the grass flat, within thirty or forty yards of where the swan was feeding. There was a big black stump there with a few small fir trees on either side of it – a perfect watching post, if I could reach it without being heard. So far as the one swan I had seen was concerned, I thought I might make it. But where were the others? Nearer or farther away? Upstream or down? One alarm note would destroy what I really wanted – the chance to watch them undisturbed in perfectly natural behaviour.

The sixty or eighty yards ahead was far more difficult than it looked. I resolved to avoid every snow patch. But where

117

there was no snow there were dry, rustling Oregon grape leaves or little willows. Big fire-blackened logs turned me or forced me to climb higher than I wanted, taller willow clumps blocked my chosen footing, the scattered snow patches seemed everywhere linked and unavoidable. But in the end I reached the stump and there had still been no alarm. Very slowly I eased my body over to one side, then raised my head. Two swans were down on the grass flat almost directly below me.

The swan I had first seen was in a little black pool of its own making, dug out in a soft place among the tussocks, feeding steadily. The other was standing several yards farther up on the flat, apparently fast asleep, neck curved back over body, the triangular base of the black bill just showing above a folded wing. The feeding swan was busy. His powerful neck plunged down, all the way in the water, driving the searching bill into the black ooze for roots and seeds. The head lifted, bill moving so that the red of the lower mandible was plainly visible. For a moment the neck, streaked with mud and dripping water, was held at full stretch while the proud head gazed sternly and alertly about. Then neck and head plunged forward again, the floating body drifting a little in recoil from the thrust and search. The movements were regular and unvarying: head down for three, perhaps four, seconds, then up and alert for exactly the same length of time, and down again.

Watching there, unseen, flooded by an excitement that satisfied every cell of mind and body, I felt an immense gratitude – to the swans, to their creator, to the little pool that had welcomed them in the frozen land and held them for me. But even as I felt these sensations I knew only too well the true source of both excitement and gratitude. These were not only the noblest and greatest of the world's wildfowl, they were also the rarest. A hundred years ago Audubon had watched "flocks after flocks" migrating along the frozen Mississippi, settling on the ice at night in hundreds, rising in the next day's dawn with a pattering of feet "that would come on the ear like the noise of great muffled drums, accompanied by the loud and clear sounds of their voice." I was watching just two, two of a few hundred remaining in the world. And I was watching these two only because the heedless, compulsive advance of men had invaded one more of their wintering sanctuaries.

The feeding swan continued his regular movements for another fifteen or twenty minutes, body and wing feathers gleaming in the clear light, their whiteness emphasized by occasional rolling drops of mud-blackened water thrown out from the raised head. Then the other swan awoke and raised its head. It stood for a moment, long neck curved gracefully over its body, then gently flapped half-open wings, and began walking slowly towards the other bird. As soon as it came close the first swan climbed easily out of his puddle and began walking ahead of his mate towards the main pool. Rather quickly they passed beyond my angle of vision, behind the stump.

I realized I was cramped and ready to move, so I straightened to my knees and worked over rather incautiously until I could see around the other side of the stump. The leading bird stopped, straightened his neck, then uttered his warning *kronk*. Now they were both alert, a little undecided but not panicky. They talked in soft, single notes, in the same key as the louder warning and always with a slight drawing down and sharp straightening of the neck. At the edge of the pool the lead bird uttered his warning again and I held the glasses on his breast and neck, trying to detect some stir from the great bugle windpipe; but I could see none – only the dip of head and neck as though to bring up the sound.

They went into the clear creek water then and at once began dipping their heads and necks to clear away the mud. The first swan was considerably the more vigorous in this, swimming strongly against the stream with neck extended just under the water until a small wave mounted over his back between his wings; then drifting slowly with the current, neck laid gracefully back over his body and swept from side to side against the feathers. It was not very successful cleaning. Both necks remained slightly streaked with the black mud or perhaps a permanent stain. But the birds seemed quickly satisfied and continued in straight-necked easy swimming with occasional gentle talk.

I had kept perfectly still, hoping they might forget about me or decide I was harmless. But they let themselves drift slowly back downstream to the first log. Here they held briefly, then turned for shore, waded out, and walked around it. They re-entered the water and drifted back to the second log, still talking a little, once or twice sounding the louder note. At the second log they waded out again, this time well up onto the grass flat. They kept on walking, rather aimlessly, so far as I could see, necks curved much of the time, but always straightening to produce the soft sounds that still reached me. One bird stretched its wings and flapped them, then both were almost still for several minutes. Quite suddenly both heads began to jerk up and down quite rapidly. A quick gabble of soft sound reached me. Then heads and necks stretched forward, wings spread, the great black feet made two or three running steps on the flat and both birds were in the air. They rose swiftly, with every strong wingbeat, climbed the steep banks of the pool, topped the alders, and swung away over the same ridge from which Alan and I had first seen them.

On the way out I followed the line of their flight and searched in the few likely places, but I did not really expect to find them again that day.

It was almost time for them to leave for the north. But these were two; a pair. The others had gone already, perhaps northward, perhaps to join the main band in the swamp at the head of the second lake. It was not too much to hope, I told myself, that these two had already chosen to stay and nest in the long pool on the open creek. It had treated them well through the winter and would treat them even better through the summer. And through the summer I would watch.

A week later I heard that the main band had disappeared from the second lake. Two or three days after that I made yet another cautious approach to the pool. It was empty. I searched the nearby beaver ponds and crossed to Hidden Lake, now free of ice. No swans. I came back to the pool, no longer cautiously. There were only the black swan holes among the tussocks of the grass flat and the fading, week-old tracks of huge webbed feet in mud or sand around them.

It is not yet April and I still hope I may find them again somewhere among the maze of swamps and beaver ponds that spring has opened. If not, perhaps it is just as well. There are too many people, too much is going on here now, for such great birds to nest in safety.

13
Little Girls and Horses
(1962)

If you have daughters and a few acres of pasture you will probably, sooner or later, have a horse or several horses. Even without the pasture you are in some danger. A recent advertisement in a Victoria paper, seeking a home for a little girl's horse, drew ninety-three offers the first day. It seems doubtful that all the prospective homes had pasture, but a good number probably had workable parents.

Except on pack trails or in cow country, horses are an anachronism. Little girls don't seem to know this, or if they do they don't care. Horses are huge creatures that eat their heads off, run up enormous feed bills, and need all sorts of loving care. Little girls understand the last part of this, but not the first. Horses need saddles and bridles and halters and ropes, and a lot of other tackle, which is perfectly all right with little girls. Horses are dangerous. If they don't kick you or bite you or throw you off, they are likely to be clumsy enough to step on you. Little girls know all this, but it seems to please them. And horses, it must be admitted, do tend to be more than normally considerate of little girls. This doesn't mean that little girls don't occasionally fall off and break their arms, or get bitten or even kicked by their horses, but it happens surprisingly seldom.

A good little girl will give her horse all the care and attention it can stand, and sometimes more. When a good little girl is at home, about all parents have to do is pay the feed bills and doctor bills and worry about the state of the pasture and the fences. But little girls go away, to school or to visit friends or for any of a number of reasons. That is when parents begin to realize why their little girls spend so much time in the pastures and out at the barn when they are home. Horses have to have water and hay and oats every day; they have to be groomed and shod and sheltered. It usually becomes evident then, too, that horses reserve all their patience and tolerance for little girls, and aren't in the least inclined to waste it on adults.

All this skirts the fact that horses may get sick and need the vet; that they may get out through fences or gates and into neighbours' gardens; that they invariably bring hordes of other little girls around, at almost any hour of the day or night, with warning of imagined calamities or urgent requests to be allowed to ride or fill the water tub or serve out some feed or even clean out the barn. A parent left in sole charge of a little girl's horse is responsible to a large and critical public.

Why are little girls allowed to have horses, then? I suppose it's something about the way they look when they ask for them, to say nothing of the number of times they will keep on asking. And there are compensations. Glance out the window some rainy spring morning after the horse has been around for a little while. You may see a long-legged daughter, still in her pyjamas, hair streaming behind as she canters the fearsome brute, without saddle or bridle, in and out among the green and pink of the apple trees. It's likely to seem reason enough on either side.

14
Ghost Cat
(1948)

North Americans generally rate the cougar as mean, vicious, and cowardly. Dozens of men, who have never seen so much as a cougar's track have expressed this view to me most emphatically. Some experienced woodsmen, despite contrary evidence, have said much the same things. Some few men I have known, sound naturalists and thoroughly experienced hunters for the most part, have expressed wholehearted admiration for the cougar's qualities, both as hunter and quarry.

I don't want to claim to be a cougar expert. I have lived in cougar country for some twenty-odd years, have hunted them a good deal and studied them closely enough to feel justified in writing one book and a few stories about them. But I have a fairly romantic and emotional approach to them and am perfectly prepared to admit it. The plain fact is that I have found them more fascinating and challenging than any other animal I have known. They are handsome and majestic creatures, superbly powerful, splendidly efficient; they are at once bold and cautious, fearful and fearless, wise and foolish, mysterious and simple.

The cougar is one of the world's medium-sized cats, larger than the bobcat or the lynx, smaller than the lion and the tiger. A well-grown male should weigh in the neighbourhood of one hundred and fifty pounds, a well-grown female around one hundred pounds. However, males of well over two hundred pounds have been recorded and mature females weighing as little as seventy pounds are not uncommon.

In superficial appearance the cougar is not unlike the African lioness, though slimmer and more graceful and with a much longer and thicker tail. The male has a wider, handsomer head than the female and gives an impression of great power in the mass of his shoulders and thickness of his forearms. Both are spotted when young and retain handsome black patches on either side of their faces and jaws. When a cougar is treed, looking down at the hunter, these are very noticeable; but the general impression of a cougar travelling on the ground is of slender, tawny-brown grace, made almost clumsy by the high hindquarters and heavy tail, yet beautifully smooth, full of confidence and power.

Cougars have been recorded from within a few miles of the Arctic Circle, clear down to the Straits of Magellan, but I have known them only in the Pacific Northwest, mainly on Vancouver Island. Perhaps the cougar's perfect range is Vancouver Island. Here are deep woods without end, tangled undergrowth, matted swamps, piled windfalls; tall mountains and rough country in abundance; and above all, deer without number – small Pacific-coast blacktails, weighing from seventy five to two hundred pounds, prey almost ideally matched to the cougar's strength and hunting skill.

Cougars are just as numerous on the Island as these almost perfect conditions suggest, yet they are rarely seen. And this is a strange thing, because they roam widely, the males especially; they seem to have an intense, bold, almost friendly curiosity about human beings and often follow a man through the woods.

Two of the most experienced trappers I have ever known, both men with over thirty years' experience on Vancouver Island, told me when I first knew them that they had never seen a cougar free in the woods. Yet both had trapped many cougars and shot others treed by dogs. And both, within a year or two of telling me that, did see cougars. Carl, who trapped alone far up the Klaanche valley, had the more dramatic experience. It was in the fall, when he was travelling back to his line. He had pitched a small tent and was lying in it half asleep one afternoon. The flaps of the tent were down and quite suddenly Carl's half-closed eyes saw them move. They moved again and Carl, fully awake, but stiffly motionless, found himself looking into the quiet eyes of a cougar, its head and one foreleg well inside the tent. Carl's rifle was down by his feet, practically under the cougar's jaws and he made no move for it until the head and paw withdrew, as quietly as they had entered.

Carl was not an excitable man and I imagine he waited a little while before moving. Then he reached for his rifle, stepped cautiously out of the tent, and saw two cougars standing within fifty feet of him. They made no move to get away but stood watching him with that calm, apparently friendly curiosity that seems so typical of cougars. Carl told me afterward that he was almost ashamed to shoot them.

Jack's cougar was a simpler affair. He saw her from the lake one day as he was passing close to shore in his rowboat – a small female, lying close against a log, watching his boat. He shot her easily, took her down in the boat to his cabin on the other lake, brought out a crock of home-brewed huckleberry wine and began to celebrate his triumph.

Quite by chance, three of us who also had trap lines near the lake decided to drop in on old Jack that night. We were all young fellows and he liked us and was always very good to us. On that particular night we were doubly welcome because we could celebrate with him. Old Jack was proud and elated as I had never seen him. By the time we got to the cabin some part of his elation undoubtedly had come from the huckleberry wine, but he made it quite clear to us, not once but many times, that he was celebrating what he felt to be the supreme achievement of a lifetime of woodcraft.

126

The wine flowed, the cougar lay in state on the floor of the cabin, old Jack rested in glory on his bunk, Jim and Alan were draped across the other bunk, and I squatted on the floor beside the cougar to examine her more closely. I picked up a forepaw, pressed the joints to force the claws from their sheaths, looked up at a sudden sharp move from Jack's bunk. Jack was on his feet, his rifle in his hands, pointed straight at me. Jim and Alan jumped for him, forced him back on the bunk and got hold of the rifle. "He don't believe me," Jack said. "He good as called me a liar, picking up that paw to look for the trap mark."

We calmed him at last and were all friends again. But that reaction is the clearest account I can give of the value that an old and thoroughly experienced woodsman set upon the achievement of seeing a cougar free in the woods. I still think that the little dead female on the floor of the cabin was the most dangerous cougar I ever had anything to do with.

The cougar's single weakness, the one thing that brings down upon him the contempt of the unknowing, is his readiness to tree for a dog. Most – but by no means all – cougars will tree very readily even for a small dog. In fact, I doubt if the size of the dog has anything to do with it. A yapping keen-hunting fox terrier or cocker spaniel is as likely to tree a cougar as the largest hound or the boldest Airedale if conditions are right – that is, if the dog has been released on a fairly fresh track and the cougar has not grown used to dogs through being hunted before.

It is difficult to account for this readiness to tree. A cougar can kill any dog on which he can lay a paw – some cougars even come down around farms and camps and small settlements to kill dogs. Certainly there is no cowardice in it, for cougars are powerful and by no means reluctant fighters. Males fight each other, occasionally to the death, over females; females fight to protect their young; both sexes will fight in defence of a kill and even the black bear, though probably not the grizzly, will give way.

It seems reasonably clear, then, that a cougar does not tree from a small dog because he is afraid of the dog, or even of the man behind the dog. I think rather that he trees from inbred habit, perhaps thousands of years old. Cougars have a very limited lung capacity and can travel at speed only for a short distance. They have always shared their range with wolves, coyotes, and other doglike animals and they must have learned long ago that trees are a safe refuge from the real dangers of big wolves or the minor irritation of yapping coyotes. I am certain that cougars feel safe when treed and I suspect that they are also a little bored – patiently waiting out a passing annoyance.

The fact that most cougars tree readily from dogs does not mean that cougars are necessarily easy to hunt down. At their own speed they are travellers of unlimited endurance and they can keep ahead of slow hounds on a cold scent indefinitely. The good hunter is the man who follows a track by his eyes rather than the noses of his dogs, keeping the dogs silent at his heels until he can release them on a really fresh scent and give them a chance to rush the cougar and quickly exhaust his lung capacity. This calls for woodcraft of a really high order and at best there is plenty of room for error – which is precisely what makes cougar hunting at least as fascinating as any other form of large game hunting.

In most large game hunting the immediate personal danger to the hunter from the hunted animal is, I believe, likely to be overrated; and when it does occur it is likely to be the result of unusual circumstances. The latter point is certainly true of cougar hunting. Shooting a cougar in a tree sounds a very simple proposition. Theoretically one catches the dogs, ties them in a safe place, selects a comfortable position to shoot from, aims, fires.

In actual practice innumerable things go wrong. Perhaps one example will be enough to illustrate some of them. The cougar, a big male, had treed just before dusk. The dogs had run on past the tree and it seemed unwise to wait to catch them. The shot would be an easy one and I moved a little way up the hill to get what seemed a clear line on the neck. It was difficult to find the sights in the dim light under the timber and just as I found them and lined them I noticed a single branch, about an inch in diameter, slanting across the cougar's neck. At the same moment I heard the dogs coming back, but I decided to take the shot, anyway. It seemed perfect. The cougar's head dropped and his forelegs drew sharply back. I ran for the foot of the tree, to be there ahead of the dogs, and could find no sign of the cougar. Just as the dogs arrived he dropped from the tree, right at my feet and very much alive. I pushed the rifle against the back of his neck and pulled the trigger. But I often wonder what might have happened if he had landed squarely on my back, because the first shot had glanced from the limb and merely nicked the point of his jaw.

But the difficulties of getting your shot at a treed cougar are as nothing to the innumerable factors that can complicate the actual hunting.

Scent can be poor, or hopelessly confused by the passing of other animals; the dogs' feet may be cut or worn raw by crusty snow or rocky ground; the best of dogs will sometimes be drawn off a good scent by coon or bear or – say it softly – deer; tracking can be intensely difficult on dry ground or after a fresh fall of snow; there may be wolves around – sure death to any dog unlucky enough to come upon them. And the cougars have their own ways of complicating things. In steep country, for instance, they will often climb a tree standing close against a tall bluff, then jump from it to the top of the bluff and leave the dogs barking confidently at the foot of the tree.

Some few cougars will run from hounds with all the cunning of the wisest fox. There was a big tom up Brown's River some years ago who seemed to know all the tricks. I hunted him several times with the great Cecil Smith, tracker without peer, but we always ended the day farther behind him than we had been at the beginning. I can remember now the last day we hunted him. We found his fresh track in good snow down in a hollow near the river. We felt certain he had killed recently and would have a full belly to slow him up and I hadn't a doubt when we turned the dogs loose that they would tree him within a quarter of a mile. They went away in fine style, two big, strong, thoroughly experienced hounds, and we followed in a hurry. Then their voices died and when we found them they were on the far side of the river. We crossed, put them on the track, and within a couple of hundred yards it took them down to the river again.

Four more times the old tom crossed the river, back and forth, and the dogs were losing their fire and we were farther behind each time. Then he went for a couple of miles up the left bank of the stream. We blundered after until we found the dogs at fault and hunting aimlessly. He had doubled back, of course, right along his own tracks for a hundred yards or so, then had cut down the slope a little way and passed back downstream within a hundred feet of us. We put the dogs on the new track and they took it keenly – back to the bank of the river again. So it went until it was too dark to hunt. We had left him, we thought, on the far side of the river. But we crossed his track again on the way out, feather fresh and heading back for where we had found him in the morning. If he hasn't died of old age he's probably still somewhere along Brown's River.

My partners, Ed and Buster Lansdowne, owned a small farm on the Nimpkish River. It was only a few cleared acres and the woods crowded close in on every side of it. Nearly always there was a cougar nearby – if we killed one, another always came to take his place and sooner or later most of them took an interest in the farm. One went right under the house to kill a favourite collie. Another, in broad daylight, trapped Mrs. Lansdowne's cocker spaniel at the edge of the river, held him under water with one paw until he drowned, then picked him up and carried him away. Mrs. Lansdowne was aboard a small boat anchored twenty or thirty feet out in the river and had to watch the whole thing helplessly – she shouted and threw things at the cougar, but he watched her calmly and completed his deliberate business without a sign of haste.

The boldest and most troublesome cougar of all, we met first on a September evening when we came in from hunting. We were hungry and sat down to a great supper in the kitchen. Somewhere, towards the end of it, there was a good deal of clucking and clacking in the chicken run. At last we strolled out there. We were inside the run before we saw him, a magnificent male cougar sitting on his haunches between the two chicken houses, a Plymouth Rock hen in his jaws.

It seemed no more than something to do, but I ran back to the house, picked up Ed's rifle and took it out to him. The cougar was still there, still calm, apparently as interested in us as we were in him. Ed took the rifle slowly. "Gosh," he said. "He's beautiful. It seems a shame to kill him."

The rest of it happened quickly and is best forgotten. The cougar moved. Ed's shot was late. The cougar was over the fence and away for the woods, the dog at his heels. He may have treed, but we didn't find him though we searched the woods till dark.

He came back for more chickens that same night, stepping around the traps we had set. I waited on the roof of the chicken house for the next two evenings and undoubtedly he watched me there because he came later, in the dark, and took more chickens. The next evening I waited on the roof of the farmhouse and he came and went through the bracken and I didn't see him.

Eventually, when most of the chickens were gone, he disappeared. A month later he was back. He evaded more traps, killed more chickens, chased the cattle in the pastures at night. We tried to pit-lamp him, but even from a hundred yards away he would only turn his great eyes to the light for a

131

fraction of a second and there was never time to put sights on him. He disappeared again for a while, then suddenly was back again. This time there was snow on the ground. He attacked a young steer in the barn and we heard the disturbance and rushed out with the rifle and a Coleman lamp. The steer burst out of the barn as Ed opened the door and knocked him over. We thought the cougar had gone out the other way and hunted him there, only to find when we came back that he must have been inside the barn all the time and slipped out when we had gone past.

The next day we hunted him grimly, but not very hopefully, following his tracks in the snow without a dog. They led us a mile or more up river, swung back, and seemed very fresh.

Then Ed had his hunch. We knew the travel of cougars on that sidehill, for we had trapped and hunted lesser beasts there. "He's going down by the big spruce," Ed said. "We can cut across and pick up his track there. It'll save time."

So we did that and by the thousandth chance that sometimes favours hunters, we met him there at the spruce tree, crouched beside the trail to let us pass unseeing. But Ed saw him and yelled and shot him as he ran.

I haven't hunted a cougar since the war and am not too sure that I want to – there are hunters enough without me and I hope there will always be cougars on Vancouver Island, lots of them. Around farms and settlements they haven't much place, but in the deep woods and on the mountains they belong. Where deer are hunted intensively cougars must be proportionately controlled. Back beyond the range of deer hunters – and most of Vancouver Island is still beyond their range – the cougar is himself a valuable control. He is also a noble creature, perfectly adapted to the country he ranges and, if the deer hunters only knew it, a quarry far more challenging to their skill and woodcraft than the little coast blacktails they hunt.

15

The Lay Mind in the Law
(1974)

Lay judges and magistrates – that is, persons without formal training in the law – have always played a major part in the administration of criminal justice. This is not surprising. Laws are usually drafted by trained lawyers, but they are or should be made for ordinary people, for the protection of ordinary people, the control of ordinary people, the peace and welfare of communities made up almost entirely of ordinary people. It follows that good laws are or should be comprehensible to ordinary people.

British Columbia has had a long history of lay judges and magistrates. The first magistrate in the colony of Vancouver Island was probably J.S. Helmcken, a medical doctor appointed to preside at Fort Rupert in 1850; he resigned a month or two later, to be reappointed in 1853. Among the first justices of the peace was also a layman, Donald Cameron, who soon after became the first Supreme Court judge and finally the first Chief Justice of Vancouver Island and British Columbia. Cameron seems to have been a great success in that even his opponents and critics agreed that he dispensed justice "not only with rigidness and exactness, but with despatch" and his judgments "exhibited prudence, firmness and candour." His greatest weakness was exactly where one would expect to find it: "in rulings during the course of a trial – rulings which must be made quickly and which require legal training and experience." Not too surprisingly, Cameron retired in 1865, after twelve years in office, and was replaced by a legally trained Chief Justice.

In the lower courts of the colony, things went differently. In 1859, soon after Judge Begbie arrived, five lay magistrates were appointed for the mainland. These men were paid respectable salaries and appear to have had extensive criminal jurisdiction. Four of the five were later appointed County Court judges and served, some with considerable distinction, until 1881.

As time went on and the province was settled, a great many magistrates were appointed. Nearly all were laymen and in the rural areas were still known as stipendiary magistrates, though the appointments carried no salaries and any financial return was limited to that provided for in the provincial and federal tables of costs. Jurisdiction was limited to summary conviction matters and the "absolute jurisdiction" section of the Criminal Code, with a strange consent area which provided that certain indictable offences could be dealt with by the magistrate after a preliminary inquiry, provided the accused consented *and* entered a guilty plea. In the larger centres there were "police magistrates" with criminal jurisdiction approximating that of today's provincial judges. These were usually lawyers, whose salaries were paid by the municipalities.

Rural and small-town magistrates and justices of the peace were appointed in the 1920s and 1930s and even later with what seems to have been almost reckless abandon. I have personally known of magistrates parked away on islands or in obscure bays and inlets who never heard a trial from the day of their appointment to the day of their death. Such appointments seem to have been made for the convenience of local citizens who needed papers signed and perhaps as a minor compliment to the appointee, as well as for the assistance of police who might want a search warrant in a hurry. I have myself recommended the appointment of justices of the peace on no more compelling grounds, though always after fairly thorough inquiries.

Once appointed, a magistrate was sent a bare-bones copy of the Criminal Code and a fairly recent edition of selected provincial statutes. After taking the oath of office, he was in business. If he was wise, he probably talked with an experienced magistrate in a nearby community, though accepting advice *with caution*. If he was curious, he soon learned that other more instructive books were available and acquired these – perhaps Snow's Criminal Code, Popple on Evidence and Popple on Procedure. If he studied these after the shock of paying for them, he rather soon realized that he knew more criminal law than a good proportion of the lawyers who appeared before him; they tended, on the whole, to be rather elderly gentlemen, more versed in wills and conveyances than in assaults and thefts. When, as occasionally happened, able and experienced criminal lawyers appeared, they were invariably considerate and helpful. The magistrate found himself eased gently over the rough spots and learning far more rapidly than books could teach.

No doubt, appointments in the thirty years since my own have been more carefully checked. Certainly many able, well-informed laymen have been appointed in British Columbia, men who have served with consistent success and sometimes distinction. But so far as I know, no effort was ever made to inform them better, to provide even minimal law libraries (apart from a subscription to the Criminal Law Quarterly and, more recently, a copy of the Magistrate's Manual) or even to suggest useful purchases. Court facilities have varied from dismal to non-existent through the 1950s and 1960s, though a few municipalities, including my own, have provided excellent physical plant and resources within the last two or three years.

The salaries of lay magistrates were always nominal, bearing little or no relationship to the services performed; any change called for degrading negotiations, usually futile. It was explained that the work was a "service to the community" and that much of the reward was the "prestige of the office": it is difficult to imagine any reward more illusory or more unwanted. I think most of us did feel that we were performing an essential and often distasteful service and, for the most part, doing it rather well. Perhaps this, too, was an illusory concept, but it kept us in operation.

In 1955, with the coming into force of the revised Criminal Code, a number of us were "specially authorized to exercise jurisdiction under Part XVI," which added very considerably to the responsibilities of the job. Later this jurisdiction was extended to all magistrates in the province. I firmly believe that this was an error scarcely short of irresponsibility. Part XVI matters arise so seldom in the more remote areas and other trials are so few that magistrates sitting there cannot possibly be expected to develop the experience necessary to perform satisfactorily with so much at stake. Sentencing, particularly, requires a sense of proportion and understanding of the possibilities that can only come with experience and careful consideration of recent precedents. I am well aware that a summary conviction trial can present difficulties as great as those of a Part XVI trial, but I am convinced that the limited "stipendiary" jurisdiction was of great value and that its removal has been the source of most of the recent criticisms of the lower courts.

I believe, very strongly, in the principle of the lay mind in the law. So, unless I misinterpret, does the great preponderance of western jurisprudence, at least in respect of the criminal law. In the most serious criminal matters, a judge alone has never been enough: he is the guiding influence in the trial and the interpreter of the law, but the jury is the judge of fact. A jury is made up of ordinary men; if the law seems unjust or unduly harsh or incomprehensible, a jury is unlikely to convict. In time, this will have its effect and the law will be changed. Juries can, it is true, be prejudiced, capricious, insensitive, or perverse. With respect, the same is true of judges, and the chances of such disabilities are greater in one man than in twelve – or so the theory goes.

There are no juries in the lower courts, but the jury principle is nevertheless there. A judge must instruct himself on the law in relation to the facts as he would instruct a jury, and having done so he becomes the jury – the judge of facts. This in itself may be an argument in favour of lay judges, albeit a tenuous one. But there is a far more important one. If the law is too difficult for the intelligent lay mind to administer, then it is altogether too difficult for most of the people upon whom it bears. If it is surrendered entirely to the triangle of lawyer judge, lawyer prosecutor, and lawyer defence counsel, it is in danger of becoming far too remote from the ordinary citizen. If legislators, too many of whom are lawyers, can depend on this, then the law is likely to become increasingly difficult and incomprehensible.

It is practically a truism that eighty or ninety per cent of the cases decided in the lower courts are decided on the facts. They require relatively little learning in the law, but call for a balanced coherent mind and the ability to listen with analytical intelligence. Case law can, of course, be helpful and some leading cases are constant guiding lights. But only rarely does a case fit exactly the case one is trying and in the end it comes down to: What do I believe and why? What do I disbelieve and for what reasons? I have often thought that the criminal statutes are far more comprehensible than some of the cases which purport to clarify them.

The lower courts – that is, the provincial courts – deal with all criminal and quasi-criminal matters and carry about ninety per cent of them to completion. They deal, at present, with all juvenile and a substantial proportion of family matters. They deal also with small claims matters between citizens. They are the courts of first resort, and they operate day in, day out, in every community. They are the citizens' courts in a very active sense. It follows that they should be as simple, straight-forward, and comprehensible as possible, that they should be prompt in giving judgment and that their reasons for judgment should be clear and concise, uncluttered by legal obscurities or learned dissertations. This is not to say that legal precedents, much less the law itself, should ever be slighted, only that these should not be allowed to obtrude or obscure; where they are essential to the judgment, their application should be plainly shown. This is counsel of perfection and perhaps rarely attainable. But at lower court levels it should be as readily attainable by articulate layman as by lawyers.

It may be asked: "How can a layman know the special applications of the law to the case before him?" A great judge once rebuked a young lawyer arguing before him in words not unlike these: "Young man, you are not to assume that I know the law. It is your duty to explain to me what you believe to be the law." Since a judge goes into court knowing nothing of the evidence to be presented by either party nor any of the issues beyond the wording of the charge itself, it is obvious that the parties involved are better informed than he is and should have a better knowledge of the applicable law. The judge must listen and decide. Only rarely should it be necessary for a lower court judge to go beyond the authorities quoted to him into broader knowledge and understanding of his own; and when it is, it simply extends the co-operation that should exist between judge and lawyers in order to arrive at an accurate interpretation.

I do not think that people who are constantly dealing with the law often realize how formidable and forbidding even the simplest court of law can seem to most of those who appear before it, whether as accused or as witnesses. The whole procedure is restrictive and inhibiting, almost entirely foreign to day-to-day living and communication. Certainly a court needs its own protections. The judge must be able to see over the courtroom, legal courtesies and formalities should be observed, proper procedure must be followed, laws of evidence adhered to. But apart from these essentials the lower courts should seek to be as informal and reassuring as possible. The objective is to get at the truth by means within the limits of the safeguards that the law provides, nothing more than this. Black robes are not necessary, a stern clerk, loud-voiced and formal, is not necessary. A prisoner's box is not necessary. Most witnesses are more at ease when seated. Apart from the necessity of a courtroom open to the public and large enough to accommodate spectators, most of the matters that come into court could as well be solved by people seated around a table. I believe that a judge who belongs to the community in which he sits can contribute something to general reassurance, and so to the search for truth.

Sentencing is difficult for all judges, laymen, or lawyers, in the lower courts and in the high courts. If it is not, the judge should take another look at himself, for something is wrong. To a very large extent the quality of sentencing must always depend on the quality of the facilities and alternatives available. It is easy enough to determine the legal limits of penalties—they are set out in plain language. One can usually keep track of the nature and quality of available facilities and check one's knowledge against the advice of probation officers and others. One can and does monitor recent Appeal Court decisions on sentencing and there is essential guidance in these. One can study books on the principles of sentencing, and there are some good ones. But with all this, sentencing must remain difficult.

Important variables always remain to be examined. No two offences are ever quite the same, nor are two offenders, two communities or two judges quite the same. A good judge will examine each of these differences faithfully and often enough the last may give him the greatest difficulty. It is not easy for a man to detect and weigh his own moral prejudices or the prejudices of his own background, but if he is fit to be a criminal judge he will try.

There is something seriously wrong with sentencing in Canada. We put far too many people in jail and keep most of them there too long, under the wrong conditions. We also release many of them under the wrong conditions. Judges can do something about this, but the real remedies are in the hands of the community and the legislators. There have been improvements and no doubt there will be more. In the meantime, reasonable sentencing calls for experience, knowledge of the alternatives, a sound sense of proportion and a recognition of shared humanity with the man in the dock. These are characteristics, acquired or innate, that are shared equally by laymen and lawyers.

The quality of a criminal court judge depends far more on the quality of the man than on the quality of the lawyer in the man. Lay judges and magistrates have served British Columbia for over a hundred years. There have been weak appointments, faulty decisions, and stupid sentences, but on the whole the service has been reasonably sound at a time and under circumstances when nothing else and no one else was available. On occasion communities have preferred to retain a lay judge when a lawyer was available and have had no cause to regret the decision.

As I have said, I believe that the principle of the lay mind in the law remains an important one. In spite of the long service of the lay judges and magistrates, I do not believe for one moment that the principle has been given a fair trial. Lay judges have been carelessly selected and given no opportunity for training. They have been grossly, in fact contemptuously, underpaid. They have had little or no access to law libraries, and have had to work in totally inadequate courtrooms, often without clerical assistance. Far too often they have had to sit without the benefit of lawyers either for the defence or for the prosecution. They have been expected to understand criminal, family, and juvenile, and sometimes small claims work equally well.

There is now every prospect of substantial improvement in

provincial court facilities. We can expect regional prosecutors responsible to the Attorney-General, court staff provided by the department and improved court facilities provided by the province instead of the municipalities. Full-time judges are now paid reasonably well and it is inconceivable that part-time and ad hoc judges, whether lawyers or laymen, will not be paid at least to the same scale. It is reasonable to hope that modest law libraries, with subscriptions to appropriate journals, will be provided wherever there is a courtroom in regular use.

One is given to understand that no laymen will be appointed to the provincial court bench in the future and that those presently serving will be "phased out" as rapidly as possible. For my own part, after more than thirty years of facing the morning docket and slighting my real profession, I should have few regrets. But I sincerely hope that this misguided idea, if it exists, will be reconsidered. A leavening of lay judges in the lower courts will always be important to the whole concept of justice.

It goes without saying that lay appointees must be selected with care, but the district judges are in a position to make a strong contribution in this process. Ideally, a short course in criminal procedure, criminal evidence, and the use of sources should be provided for all newly appointed judges. Failing this, a prospective judge should sit with an experienced judge for a month or two before taking up his own duties. In either case, he should then be required to serve an apprentice period, perhaps six months or a year, with powers limited to summary conviction matters and the absolute jurisdiction section of the Criminal Code. The rest is experience, and this requirement is much the same for both laymen and lawyers.

It is necessary to say again that the lower courts are courts of first resort. Most people who come before them want decisions that are prompt, just, binding, and comprehensible. Promptness at this stage is a significant part of justice itself. Major points of law do not often arise at this level and are never settled there. When a significant point of law does arise, the appeal courts are readily available should either party feel aggrieved by the lower court decision. A certain input of lay minds can be of advantage in this as in all stages of lower court performance. The law is much too important to be left solely to lawyers.

16

An Outsider Looks at Education
To the Vancouver Island Teachers
(1950)

It is a very real honour for me to be here tonight, and paradoxically the more so because I am here as an outsider, not as an educator. My family has been closely connected with education for over a hundred years. My grandfather was a famous headmaster and administrator in England. My father was a teacher, and, in proportion to his brief time in the work, almost as well known. I have many uncles, aunts, cousins, and other relations, who are or have been schoolteachers. I myself am a back-slider. I never taught anybody anything. So I am allowed to speak to you here tonight as a layman, an ordinary citizen, someone whose interest in education is only direct, not professional.

I do not want to convey to you by all this that I never went to school. I did. In fact I spent many uneasy years there and faced many teachers, though never as many as I am facing tonight. I liked some of them, and was a trial to others, as I probably shall be tonight. But in the end, I learned to read and write and went on out into the great world. For many years I had little to do with schools and schoolteachers. Then I became a parent of schoolchildren. I now have three children in school and another on the way there. Short of going to school oneself, that is probably the most intense concern anyone can have with school. So I speak to you tonight as a father of schoolchildren.

I speak to you also as a magistrate and a juvenile court judge, and therefore as one intimately concerned with the yield of your system.

And I speak as a citizen, devoutly hopeful for the future of Canada and the world, and deeply conscious that this future depends very largely on what happens in the schools. So you will have to forgive me if I speak without the diffidence and humility that might be proper in an outsider.

For better or worse, this country is committed to public education. We have private schools, but they are few and small and their influence, it seems to me, is little felt either in the Department of Education or in the country's life, though it is significantly more noticeable in the latter than the former.

Personally, I am content with this situation. It is an experiment, probably the greatest and most dangerous experiment democracy has yet tried. But it is also an inevitable development; democracy has to develop into public education, has to succeed in it – or else die out and let something else grow up in its place.

The greatest advantage of public education is that it provides equality of opportunity, insofar as schooling makes opportunity. It also ensures an overwhelmingly literate population, if by literate we mean "able to read and write." And it sets a new pattern of life in that home life and school life are, or should be, always integrated never separate. Through this it ensures that all the variations of society are brought together in daily touch with one another through a long, formative period.

These are significant advantages, and the combination of home and school life is not the least of them. No boarding school can give the moral and intellectual training that a good home can give, in combination with a good day school. The realistic, day by day atmosphere of a home is by itself an

144

important factor in training for life. The artificial segregation of the boarding school may have some advantages in developing a child; but they are not comparable to those that a home can provide.

All this, then, is on the credit side of public education. I have said that this is democracy's most dangerous experiment. Let me outline some of the dangers.

It is my conviction that all government is evil. It may be a necessary evil, or the evil may be materially limited, but government remains evil because it is the delegation or assumption of powers over individual citizens by a group, large or small. It can be benevolent, even constructive and creative, but the inherent evil still remains. It is a reduction of the individual for the sake of the mass.

I say this only to emphasize a tendency. Clearly we have to have government and we intend to have government. But in handing to government anything so precious as full responsibility for the education of our children, we have to remember that we are handing enormous power, practically complete power, to an organization invariably and inevitably corrupted by power.

There is a tendency in all government affairs to bureaucratic stiffness and blindness. There is a tendency to mass production, to system and tidiness. An inclination to accept mediocrity as normal and desirable. An instinct towards stagnation, laziness, and time serving. And, most serious of all, in a democratic government there is a natural readiness to yield to the wishes, prejudice, bad taste, and ignorance of the mass mind that produces the mass vote.

These are evils enough to make a mockery of every purpose of education. Unchecked they would destroy democracy within a few generations. They may be doing so now; some people believe they are. I do not and I am certain there is no such deliberate intent. But I think we are endangered by all of these things, that our nation and our way of life are endangered by them. And I believe that they are progressive and cumulative in effect, more subtle than the most pernicious of revolutionary doctrines. Their fruit is stagnation, decay, and decadence.

The remedy, as most of us have been taught from our cradles, is in ourselves. It is our duty and our right, individually and collectively, to think, to understand, to speak out and force our government to make proper use of the powers we have delegated. In an older day, when the private schools had power and authority, they could give leadership in this. Now the leadership can come only from a lay public; unless it comes, as it should come, from the teaching staffs of the public schools and universities. In other words from yourselves.

It is that duty and privilege that I want to emphasize to you above all others tonight. It is yours and you cannot escape it. Your future stands or falls by your performance of it; the future of the nation stands on this and the future of the free world. And I am not exaggerating or dramatizing the thing by any shade of meaning.

You are educators, not civil servants or businessmen or mere wage earners. To educate means to lead forth. It may mean to lead a child forth from the animal ignorance of childhood; it may mean to lead forth from the child the great and complicated humanity that is his potential. Either task is a heavy responsibility, a matter for creative effort, not for routines and set theories. While you can serve democracy as almost no one else can, yours is not a democratic function. It is a function of power, authority, dignity; and you are leaders, dominies, masters, preceptors. You cannot be any of these things unless you are thinking men and women, people of inquiring and questioning minds, accepting nothing that is handed down to you without closest examination; you must be constantly seeking for yourselves mental growth; you must never accept the easy way, the blind way, the dead way of followers of bureaucracy, because you deal in human lives, in the collective life of the nation, not in constants and statistics. If you hold to all this, government control will never be a danger – and no Minister of Education will ever sleep calmly in his bed.

So far I have spoken in generalities. I want now to look at the thing more closely and concretely. Public education is big business; it is probably this continent's largest industry – two people out of seven in North America spend their working lives on matters of education. Enormous sums of money are being spent. Schools and universities have been and are being built on a scale never before imagined. Taxes for education are enormous. Children are studied, theories are developed, teaching methods are stylized and defined. Everything is hygenic and streamlined and compound-worded into an unbelievable semblance of efficiency.

Personally, I doubt the efficiency. I believe that far too much money is going into fine buildings and filing systems and public address systems and road transportation and specialized courses that have little or nothing to do with education.

Fine buildings do not necessarily mean a fine education. Up to a point they can help, but that is all. Transportation, and most of the machinery of administration, is sheer waste, and I doubt we can or should afford either on the scale in which we have it. One thing, and one thing only, ensures first-rate education, on the level that is vital to the survival of a democracy; and that is fine teaching, teaching based on true depth of knowledge and understanding.

It is obvious that the people of Canada and the United States can outproduce, materially, the bravest dreams of all the world's thinkers. Economically, mechanically, scientifically we have a civilization such as the world has never seen. The question is: Do we know what to do with it? The civilization that produced these economic advances was not built in a day, nor in a thousand years. The civilization that can handle them without being overwhelmed by them must be a continuing development of the civilization that produced them. And this continuation must be in and through the schools, more than anywhere. Not in the buildings, nor in the syllabus, nor in the mechanical aids, but in the teaching. It will not be in a teacher's precise knowledge of the course he is teaching, nor in his surface efficiency as a teacher; but in the *depth of background and understanding from which he is teaching*, in the whole quality of man or woman that the teacher is. This always has been and always will be.

To return for a moment to buildings and the concrete appurtenances of teaching – frills, some people call them. It is nothing to find half a million dollars for a new central school in a small district. Nothing to find thousands for a cafeteria, a home economics room, a workshop, an auditorium. Nothing to find thousands annually for school buses. Yet it is considered the most normal thing in the world to build such a school without budgetting the ten thousand dollars needed to give the school a basic library. So normal, in fact, that no one ever remarks on it, except the children.

What, I wonder, are we trying to do? I can see that books, apart from carefully emasculated textbooks, might be a dangerous thing to have in a sterilized modern school. Books are full of ideas, and some of the ideas might be quite upsetting to the routines of the curriculum. But I'm going to make a very venturesome statement. Books are pretty good things. In fact a school without a decent library is an educational shell. Education that does not expose children to books, does not force them to books and teach them to explore freely and vigorously among them, is a fraud. An educated person, within the meaning of school and university training, is simply one who is ready to go ahead and learn for himself. Sixteen years of the best in mechanical equipment and hygenic teaching methods can fail dismally to teach this. Six or eight years with access to books, and a dash of inspiration thrown in with the teaching, has often been enough. Education is still book learning, and always will be. It is the unlocking of the world's knowledge, stored in books, to a mind trained to understand and use it. Much must always depend on the quality and responsiveness of the individual who is being taught. But I believe that today's system leaves many who have the necessary qualities unawakened and untaught.

There is a saying in biology that the history of the individual recapitulates the history of the race. Each human embryo passes through stages that recall evolution through fishes, through tailed creatures and furred creatures to man. It is even truer to say that the individual mind must recapitulate the history of its civilization before it can be considered educated. I have tried to say already that democracy is not a safe or a static thing. It is of its nature progressive, dynamic, full of change and growth. But it is informed and intelligent change, cumulative growth, a building on sorted and collected wisdom. Its progression is the sane progression of thinking men and women, not the abrupt cleavage from the past and the fearful waste of human wisdom that is revolution. Change of this sort, the sort that keeps democracy alive and gives it its only hope of permanence, is built not by governments, but by the individual, creative thought of millions of men and women. The failure of any significant proportion of these millions of people can mean the failure and destruction of the whole.

I believe that this power of individual, creative thought is overwhelmingly the most important thing that the schools must teach. And they cannot afford to fail with any child capable of learning. If the system is to succeed and go on, there must be teaching success, in this sense, with a higher and higher proportion in every generation.

No child can develop to play its part successfully in a nation conceived as ours is unless it learns and understands, not merely the superficialities of its civilization, but the whole, long derivation of the social structure. This is not a new conception of education. It is one of the oldest. It is the one that has developed our own civilization. It is the only realistic one. And it is one that has been almost lost in the shallow, easy,

149

attractive theories of education that grew from Columbia University in the early years of this century.

Sometimes, watching my own children, knowing that two of them have already chosen to follow the hard way of classical scholarship, I feel safe in them. I find myself thinking that they have chosen, not really the hard way, but the easy and safe way, perhaps the only way, to a life as creative individuals. Among a generation of specialists, they will be part of an intellectual aristocracy, akin to the clerks of the Middle Ages, keeping civilization alive, knowing their world, living as men and women, not machines. But I know I am crazy to think this. I know in my heart that there is neither safety, nor survival, nor progress in any isolated aristocracy.

This civilization is based on many civilizations – Egyptian, Jewish, Greek, Roman, Saxon, French, to name a few of them. Its roots are in Roman law and Saxon law and British law. In Greek culture, in the Latin language, in English and French and Russian and North American literature. It is in the Norman Charters and the Tolpuddle martyrs and modern trade unionism. Above all it is rooted, set, guided, and inspired by Christianity, which in turn grew from the magnificent Jewish conception of one God.

Not all these things can be clearly shown to a child in twelve brief years of schooling. But the way to understanding them must be opened, and it can be opened only by teachers who themselves understand, teachers who are scholars and readers and individuals, not merely mouthpieces of a set curriculum.

I have said that the integration of home life and school life is one of the most valuable yields of public education. I should have said: it once was, it now could be and should be. We inherited on this continent the yield of generations raised in Christian ethics. And we have coasted on it. Recognizing the violence and diffusion of sectarian quarrels, we were guided by some half wisdom into excluding religious teaching from the schools. Let religion, we said, be taught in the home, and keep the schools for less disputatious matters.

This might have been well enough – had religion been taught in the homes. What we forgot was that in some homes it inevitably would not be taught. And that those homes would then raise, as inevitably, children utterly ignorant of Christianity, though living in a society based on Christian ethics. We forgot also that in every successive generation, with the inevitability of biologic recession under Mendel's Law, there would be more and more families raising more and more children in utter ignorance of the foundations of their morality.

Christianity is an enormous historical fact, probably *the* greatest single historical fact. Without understanding of it, everything taught and everything lived is without frame, almost without meaning. I seriously question whether anyone who has not a good knowledge of the contents of the Bible, both Old and New Testaments, can be considered educated in the terms of western civilization. Yet we have left this matter to chance.

I want to say in all seriousness that no church, no state, has the right to deny its children clear and powerful instruction in the facts of Christianity; that these facts are an integral part of all learning; that morality, in the sense of our times and our society, becomes a matter of chance without such instruction. I want to say that in the name of religious freedom we are destroying not only religion itself, but the validity of everything we try to teach.

In somewhat the same way, at the behest of the defeatist cynicism of the twenties and thirties, under the bankrupt anachronisms of Marx and Engels, and their thousands of successors, we have thrown patriotism out of the window. I do not want to deny the greatness of Marx. He was needed and some of the things he said were needed when he said them. But, partly because he said them, far more through its own dynamic flexibility, our civilization changed into courses of which he never dreamed, and left much of his teaching

151

without meaning. And the bitterness of his mind set out to destroy many things of more real and lasting value than anything he taught. Patriotism is one of these.

Patriotism is no evil thing. It can be used for evil, as anything, even Christian teaching, can be used for evil. But in honourable use it is wholly good, and no reasoning can make it otherwise. Every man who accepts the idea of an organized society owes loyalties – to himself, to his family, his community, his province, his nation; and now at last to something approaching a world federation. All these loyalties are interdependent. None can exist to the full without the others. Most of the world's great human tragedies, nearly all human triumphs, have revolved around the ordering and reconciliation of these loyalties. A completely honourable man is one who gives to each loyalty its full value, and slights none of them. And a completely honourable man is not created without teaching. By the same token, no man can learn the larger loyalties except through the more intimate ones. Loyalty to family, to school, honest, thinking loyalties, are the necessary prerequisites of patriotism. Faith in one's own country, love of it to the point of unsparing effort, is the only means by which man can fit himself for loyalty to his brothers everywhere.

I have spoken at length of these things, because they become trite and meaningless phrases unless one does examine them closely, and assess their value against the perspective of modern living. I believe that the function of a school is to develop in a child the capacity to understand its world and become a thinking part of it. It is not the business of a school to train a child to do a job or earn a living – that is for later living, and there is no time for it in school years. A school must teach the fundamentals of useful living – mathematics, elementary science, and the use of the English language; this last, above all – but its main function must be, through this means, to develop a capacity for understanding and further learning.

I have learned, in court, that it is possible for a child to go through high school without knowing the story of the gospels. I have learned, through friends who teach at universities, that it is possible for a child to come into freshman English without ever having read through a book. Only the other day I heard two doctors who teach in medical school complaining that students come to them still unable to express themselves in written or spoken English and unable to read intelligently. Instead of these obvious requirements, they have smatterings of science that have to be unlearned.

Twenty or thirty years ago there was, perhaps, room for argument about these things. A new day had dawned. Education, it seemed, could be simplified, reduced to system, streamlined into foolproof simplicity. That time has long passed and the emptiness of the system is apparent. But the time is now short. Western democracy has to understand itself, hold to its deepest meanings, give them new and richer meanings. It has raised a generation of machines, a generation of men and women who do not know "what manner of people we are." We have raised a Fuchs, an Allan Nunn May, and thousands like them, minds capable of the ultimate in specialized thought, yet morally, politically, and intellectually so uneducated, so inept that they are utterly unfitted for any sort of trust. Such grandiose failures as these are symptomatic of other failures all through the population. They show all too clearly that a *human* education is an essential of decent performance in life.

What in all this is my quarrel with teachers? Directly, nothing. Within the limited framework they have accepted for themselves they are conscientious, loyal, sincere, and competent. Indirectly, my quarrel is with every acceptance by a teacher of limits to his scope. It is that teachers, too, have let themselves become specialized machines, spokesmen for system, administrators, servants of the state, instead of scholars and leaders and rounded human beings. It is that the profession is nowhere near realizing its potentialities, that it does

153

not begin to make the creative contribution it should to the life of the nation.

It fascinates me to notice again and again at teachers' conferences discussion of the prestige of the profession. Perhaps that is a family matter, upon which an outsider should not venture. I must admit that every time I see the thing mentioned in this way I feel embarrassment. Yet it clearly is a matter for outsiders, because the teachers who speak in this way are saying that they do not feel the respect of the community.

Prestige, ladies and gentlemen, cannot be whistled up or legislated. It will not grow out of crying for it or asking for it. Prestige follows quality, as night follows day; follows performance, as a river follows its channel; and in the last analysis. it must always follow the man, not his profession. Only when many men have performed well in a profession, over a long period, with devotion, integrity, power and skill and depth, does the profession itself begin to draw prestige. And the moment this happens the profession itself enters danger. Prestige is never secure, never automatic, never good for a man or a profession if either takes it seriously.

Any discussion of professional prestige naturally turns thought to the medical profession. In a matter of a hundred years, doctors raised their profession from its doubtful status among barbers, leeches, sorcerers, witches, and medicine men to a peak of respect. They did it by creative performance, by devotion, by working long hours, often to ill health and death, and by maintaining ethical standards that made no compromise with the highest service that could be attained. They accepted long, difficult, and expensive training and they worked always from a body of knowledge whose total was seldom called into play. Out of this, and out of the human need for doctors, has come the prestige and the financial rewards often associated with the profession.

These rewards are now a danger to the profession. They

attract people who are interested in little else. Fortunately the way to becoming a doctor is still long and hard, the standards are still high. But the profession must guard itself far more carefully than in the days when its prestige was less obvious and less universal.

Teachers are even more important to the community than doctors. The scope of their profession is, or should be, greater. Its requirements should be as exacting and far more complex. Teachers have often reached towards these things, but they have never, as a whole profession, quite grasped them. I believe that the normal workings of state education, by preferring obedient civil servants to creative individuals, throttles not merely the profession's hope for itself, but the whole broad meaning of education.

We have in British Columbia a state university. It would seem the simplest logic to use it to train teachers to a breadth of knowledge and understanding that would make them a truly powerful influence. Instead, we force them to plough through twelve or fifteen long years of summer school towards the degree that should free their minds for real development. It is not my purpose tonight to examine the administrative problems that would be raised by subsidizing prospective teachers through university, but I am sure that none of them is insoluble or even difficult. And I am sure that nothing would pay greater dividends to the country.

This would be a start, and a long one, towards the sort of education a progressive democracy deserves. But there are many other essentials, nearly all of them concerned with teachers and teaching. I think reasonable permanence is essential to good teaching and to the development of good teachers. A teacher should grow and develop within a single school and move on only when his development makes him fit better elsewhere. Out of this permanence would come far better schools, schools with character and meaning; and far better teachers with loyalty and purpose and stability, a sense

155

of growing and belonging instead of everlastingly adjusting. It would also enable a community to know its teachers well enough to learn respect for them.

To be an adequate professional, whether doctor or lawyer, teacher or writer, a man must live his profession twenty-four hours a day, relentlessly. The eight-hour day is not and never will be for the creative and constructive professions. A teacher must never cease to grow, not merely in teaching technique, but in depth of knowledge from which to teach. No lifetime will ever be long enough for a man to perfect himself as a teacher. No matter what his subject, there will always be new facets of it to be examined; he can, and must, always work on to round himself and build himself; he must fit all knowledge that comes to him into the whole knowledge from which he teaches. Only through this can he ever hope to pass on to others the strength and honesty of wisdom they will need as citizens of a democracy.

Somewhere from this, the prestige of the profession will grow, will come unsought for. And, what is far more important, out of this will come the only sure survival and growth of the system we all love and believe in. Teachers who are themselves powerful and honourable individuals will build schools that have meaning. From such schools, built of teaching, not lumber and plaster and concrete, will grow humans who can continue the slow, solid, always richer flowering of their race. There is no finer cause.

17
Choice for Canadians
Security or Freedom
(1954)

Material security is a fine thing. It can make for stable families, well-adjusted children, reasonable contentment, and the sort of cushioned lives that most people feel they need. A good measure of it, through family allowances, old age pensions, veterans' pensions, government and private pension schemes of many kinds, unemployment insurance, and ready social assistance, is undoubtedly needed to maintain the modern industrial economy of produce and use and throw away.

Certain other merits are claimed for it, notably that it makes men free to think and talk and develop into the positive individuals that a democracy needs. Of these claims I am much more doubtful. Security, like anything else, has its price, and the price is not payable in taxes alone. Security is a stifling and deadly thing for many people. The idea of it grips their minds in the schoolroom, limits them in choice of university training, grooves and patterns their working lives, gently eases them into the second-rate satisfactions of shiny mass production, and eventually plants them in well-kept graves after a lifelong illusion of life. So far from having lived as free and constructive citizens, they will have paid unceasing tribute to all the second-rate satisfactions dreamed up for them – superficial knowledge, bad taste in art and entertainment, false standards in personal conduct, and a narrow, distorted view of the world they have passed through.

When all this is said, the moderate security of the industrial welfare state remains infinitely preferable to the poverty, exploitation, squalor, and ignorance of most civilizations that have preceded it. No doubt virtuous simplicity and rugged honour existed under these conditions, as they do today; but they were wrapped in physical miseries that can have done little to increase the stature of mankind, and in hereditary distinctions between man and man that were false and founded in meanness of spirit. At least the industrial state has living seeds of growth and freedom in it, and it can place within physical reach of man, any man, the things his soul should seek. If it obscures them from him with the glossy froth of its own waste, it still offers more than its predecessors.

But without rebels and sports, such a state is bound to die. Canada could die very easily, before she is fairly born, under the sheer weight of short-lived automobiles, the welter of shoddy entertainment, and the burden of a time-serving, pension-conscious citizenry.

Fortunately, human social organizations don't work that way. In seeking to favour one group, however large or small, they invariably foster a new group that reaps the real advantage. The age of chivalry made things easy for the merchant prince. The French Revolution built an elegant bourgeois state. The Russian experiment in a classless society, if there is anything in reports, has raised a supreme tyrant, supported by an oligarchy of ruthless lieutenants, who are served in turn by a petty aristocracy of bureaucrats. The welfare state, or at least that version of it current in North America, offers most to those bold citizens who disregard security at every turning point of their lives – and it stands to gain most from them.

The pattern of security is not really new. Every respectable Victorian parent urged his child into a "nice, steady job, with

158

prospects," and seems to have been disregarded as often as not, at least by those who left a mark. The famous Depression of the thirties made the big change. Those of us old enough to start our working lives in the bright world just before it, have usually held to our old, improvident ways, sure that having survived once we shall survive again. But somehow, probably by dramatizing our early difficulties, we bred a race of children with wary eyes for the economic weather. And we quickly hedged them round with all the temptations and limitations of the incipient welfare state.

We declared it an age of specialization, a time when most jobs are so complicated that learning must start early and life must be grooved into them. Industry was ready to go along with that, so was labour, so was the state. And so were the children. You named it in high school and began preparing there, selected an appropriate university course, went from that to the job and presumably followed safely on through nicely graduated promotions to an early pension. It is a useful pattern for an industrialized, urban civilization, which is exactly why it has been allowed to develop. But it doesn't make for first-rate satisfactions or first-rate people.

This may or may not be all right for finding new oil wells, building new factories and running everything more or less efficiently. But there is an enormous amount of work to be done and service to be given in a new nation – or an old one, for that matter – which has little to do with material production. The children in school and university today, and probably their children after them, are going to have a great deal to do with setting the ways of Canada, building her national life, creating her art and literature and music, forming her laws, establishing the quality of service she will give her own people and the rest of the world.

These things cannot be well done, and some of them cannot be done at all, by minds limited by specialized education for specialized jobs, for whom security and conformity are guiding principles. They will be done, as always, by people who sense in themselves a capacity to reach for the infinite and the undefined, by people who know, if they bother to think about it at all, that their only security is in their own worth and that every compromise they make for security reduces their worth.

There is no formula for producing such people. They come from farms and factories and the woods, from city streets and highly-priced residential areas and forgotten fishing villages. But the times can encourage them and educators can watch for them and parents can bear with them – perhaps even suffer a little for them. For they are the people who do unlikely and unpredictable things, the people who give body and life and meaning to a nation.

It is absurdly difficult to point to the sort of people I am thinking of, except by saying they are people who not only fill, but overflow whatever jobs they do, people who bring to their lives as well as their jobs a breadth and generosity and devotion that doesn't shut off with an eight-hour day and is never ready to go to pension. One may be a railroad conductor who is known to everyone in the length of his run and somehow makes it mean much more than that. Another may be a teacher who has watched forty years of changing faces without a slackening of interest. Still another may be a painter who has kept his vision clear and bright through five or fifty years of poverty. It doesn't matter very much who they are or where they are; their quality is what they do and give.

Performance that rejects security is everywhere, but when I search for examples I think of the young lawyer who takes his learning and inexperience out to a small town, to practise criminal law, draw up contracts and wills, listen to people's troubles, give you advice and whatever else he is asked for, instead of settling to a profitable lifetime of divorce court practice in the city. I think of the young doctor or priest who goes out to a mining settlement in the sincere conviction he is needed there. I think of the boy who has just left high school and works with a survey crew instead of where the pay is bet-

160

ter "because there's a chance to learn something."

But the same thing can happen in a million other ways and a million other lives. It's no use trying to call it, but it is important not to stifle it, because it can mean an urgency of life and happiness that no amount of security can ever give. To my own children I say: "By all means learn to do something useful but take the broadest education you can find, fit everything you know into it, and everything else you learn into the total. And don't stop learning."

The reason I tell them this is because I believe there are absolute standards of value, at least within the framework of the civilization we are trying to build, and that there is enough stored-up human wisdom by which to learn to judge them. There is a clearly detectable difference between the first-rate and the second-rate in everything that is of the slightest importance – in the arts and in literature, in politics and in law, in religious teaching and secular teaching, in human lives and human performance.

It is important for Canada that she should have an abundance of citizens who will constantly question everything about her – government, industry, art, education, the church, the judiciary, public services, their own lives and their own jobs – by first-rate standards. Ultimately these same citizens are going to have to ask themselves the most difficult and important question of all: "How can Canada behave humanely and wisely and safely in her dealings with the rest of mankind?" If they don't find the right answer to that, by first-rate standards, the security of the welfare state and the shiny yield of the industrial state will have little meaning for anyone.

18

The Quality of Living
(1970)

Until very recently, only the favoured few in any society have had time to question seriously the quality of living. Life itself, survival enhanced by a few occasional pleasures, kept most people fully occupied. This questioning by the few was, more often than not, itself of very high quality and impressively productive. It was the yield of leisure, acquired either by wealth or by determination – the time to think.

Today, for the first time in history, very large numbers of people have not only the time to think but substantial training in the processes of thought and the real material of thought. In western civilization, leisure is no longer the privilege of the few; it is, in substantial degree, a part of life for everyone. Education to capacity is the rule rather than the exception. And the prospect is for continuing advances in both fields.

This extraordinary achievement, based on human institutions and ingenuity and on the riches of the earth, satisfies almost no one. It is, of course, still incomplete, still inequitable and uncertain, and these are legitimate matters for dissatisfaction. But the dissatisfaction goes far beyond such obvious issues to question the direction of education, the uses of leisure, the responsibilities of the individual, the sanctity of institutions, the purpose of living. This is not new. What is new is that the questioning is not confined to the philosopher's study or the scholar's cloister. It is actively in the minds of many people, especially younger people, and it finds ready and powerful (though often ephemeral) means of expression.

It is easy to say that much of the questioning reflects leisure rather than learning, and there's some truth in this. But it has been obvious for many years now – at least forty years that I am aware of – that the leisure has been coming and society should be getting ready to welcome it and provide for it. On the whole, society has done neither, so the present questioning is both important and urgent.

The quality of living is an individual matter. We can agree on certain essentials – air clean enough to breathe, water clean enough to drink, a fertile and productive earth, warmth enough to survive against the elements, and some minimal ration of sunlight for the spirit. This consensus is the source of our belated concern with environmental quality; it has overtones of the universal animal concern for survival and on that basis can affect even the least sensitive. More realistic concepts, such as the integral nature of the planet and the interdependence of all life, are as yet far from universal understanding or acceptance. Yet there is no doubt in my mind that they have a very great deal to do with the quality of human living. It may just be possible for the human race to defy them and survive, but it would be an inferior survival of a lessened species.

For many people, there is a rich quality of life in ordinary, day-to-day human associations, often within a very narrow frame – that of a city enclave, a small town or a village. They find fulfillment in this and ask no more. Others can focus on a single institution, dedicate a life to it, and die fulfilled. Most of us ask a little more and reach a little farther.

I think it is safe to say that life has no purpose other than that discovered in it or given to it by the individual. Until recently the common prescription was: "get a job and do it well," or "learn a craft and master it." Given some such central focus and the incidentals inevitably surrounding it, life could be full and satisfying. To some extent this remains true today. But, except in certain fields, jobs have become less demanding of both time and energy, and craftsmanship has been taken over by machines; at the same time people, through leisure and education, have become more demanding of themselves and their lives. So we begin to question the quality of the life that seems to be available to us.

We cannot question seriously or effectively without reference to the past. Without the past there is no future for man, nor even a present being. All he is is the sum of his past, and all he can hope to become is written somewhere in this experience. To know the past is not necessarily to be bound by it, but some degree of knowledge can save a lot of wasted effort and set a frame for performance that gives life the meaning of shared human endeavour.

The past of man is not necessarily confining. It has never been static. Much has been learned and discarded. Much has been accumulated, tested, and refined. Whatever has been so tested and refined is not to be easily discarded, though it can and should be questioned and retested. No generation is sufficient unto itself; it is merely an incident in the life of mankind, which is itself only an incident in the life of the planet and a speck of dust in the history of the universe.

Against this awesome backdrop of space and time, against man's own history of striving and learning and knowledge, the search for quality in living is a search for individual identity and sense of worth – a supremely bold and perhaps specifically human undertaking. One can afford to inject it with a small measure of humility and some respect for the achievement of the past.

In the past the major emphasis of man's effort has gone into production – the primary production of the hunter, the fisherman, the grower, the miner, the forester, and the secondary production of the craftsman, the builder, the manufacturer. Today proportionately much less human time goes into production, much more into service of all kinds, from the servicing of automobiles to the serving of human souls. Education, government, law, medicine, social work, are all massive fields of service that can contribute as much to the welfare of the individual as production, if only because the yield of production is meaningless if its benefits are not properly distributed.

This is something that government and educators, even lawyers and doctors, have been slow to understand, even though ordinary people have sensed it long ago. Understanding it, providing properly for it, developing a practical philosophy to guide it, may well be the key to the quality of life that so many of us feel is escaping us, in spite of our obvious material welfare.

In the confusion of values, in the new uncertainties of leisure and partial education, lacking guidance and leadership, many young people have turned to flight and evasion. Communes and little Utopias may be temporary refuges, but they cannot provide an adequate quality of living, nor can they survive for very long, for many good reasons, not the least of which is human nature and personality. But in another sense, as a simple means of teaching an individual's relationship with the natural order, they can have value. And there is a distinct possibility that one of their effects may be to modify the shift to urbanization.

The real quality of living is not to be found in drugs, precisely because it *is* to be found in their opposite: the sharpening of innate perception and sensitivity. I am aware that this is still a controversial subject, but no one who has observed the dead eyes and listened to the flat voices of the child-users can have serious doubts that drug effects are negative. Potential is contracted, not expanded. Life and living are dulled and deadened, not stimulated, revealed, or revitalized.

The quality of living has not been enhanced by the so-called sexual revolution or by unqualified freedom in theatre, film, and literature. This surprises me more than a little. The new freedoms have, of course, been clumsily and awkwardly used and often outrageously exploited. Dishonesty and superficiality have displaced the frankness and innocence that were predicated. The result has been that the sense of uniqueness and intimacy that made sexual experience the most intense of human relationships has been significantly degraded. This is life reducing rather than life enhancing. Yet I believe that the choice of freedom is a sound one. Experience will guide its use and purpose and restore a valid sense of proportion. In time the new attitudes and new freedoms will be used with intelligence and restraint. When this happens, they will add to the quality of life.

I have suggested that what we want of life is a sense of individuality and a sense of worth. Many people have rejected the traditional satisfaction and doubtful prestige of material possessions. Many have not, and for these there is perhaps no problem – getting and spending, "the good life," will suffice for at least a little longer. But the future is with the others and it is those we are concerned with in this present discussion.

If there is a common denominator in this search for a life of meaning and quality, it is this: a desire to work with people and for people, either directly or in such a way that the effort is plainly dedicated to the ideal. It is a people-oriented rather than a profit-oriented philosophy and by extension is concerned with life, all living things, rather than inanimate objects. Young people often express it very simply in this form: "I want to help other people."

It is perfectly arguable that one is helping others by simply working in a factory and turning out newsprint or trucks or washing machines – after all, the world's work has to be done. It is also arguable that this does not make a full or satisfactory life. The work is often physically and mentally undemanding, it offers little scope and almost no variety. It does, however, provide fairly good wages, quite regularly, the hours are short and likely to grow shorter, the individual is left with time and energy for other things. A number of young people have already recognized the opportunities that exist in this situation and have found ingenious ways to put their surplus time and energy to good use. But it is a field that deserves the further study of educators and much wider recognition by society as a whole.

The ideal of service is a good one, but one is often tempted to ask the young man who wants to help others: "What have you got to offer – other than a sense of superiority? How have you prepared yourself?" The answers are not likely to be satisfactory. Helping people directly with the problem of their daily lives is usually a slow, exacting, repetitious business that yields vague and uncertain results. Social workers and priests do it, in direct line of duty and often far beyond that. Lawyers and doctors do it, because their work brings them many troubled people. Schoolteachers and counsellors may do it on occasion. Judges, court clerks, and policemen do it all the time, again because their work brings them troubled people, but also because they are obvious sources of experience and seemingly clothed with authority. Barmen do it, for much the same reasons. Nearly all educated people find themselves doing it at one time or another. Yet all of this still falls far short of the need, and it is placing an increasingly heavy burden on a few skilled or trained people. It is one of the facts of our civilization that this burden will go on increasing to intolerable levels unless something is done to recognize the need it fills. As the standard of living continues to rise and ordinary working hours continue to be reduced, the demands on the time, energy, and efforts of professional, trained, or merely experienced people, will continue to grow.

This, then, can be seen as a demand for service of precisely the type that the underemployed intellectual could readily be trained to give. Many people are already living greatly enriched lives as teachers' aides. There is room for much more

167

semi-professional work of this nature in many fields, though much of it would require some minimum of training. Consider only the field of law. Many students go through seven years of schooling and a year of articles, to emerge ill-equipped to argue a simple case in criminal court. It is not surprising. The field of law is vast, complicated, and endlessly confusing. Criminal law is a small part of it, not a lucrative part and not a highly respected part. Yet criminal lawyers are very much needed. I believe that any competent arts graduate, given a year's special training in criminal law and procedure, could come into court a worthy and well-equipped advocate. No doubt there are other branches of law where a period of specialized training would ensure sound performance; and a period of specialized practice need not prevent a man returning for further training to broaden his field. He would certainly return as a much more apt and receptive student.

I could extend this argument even in the field of law – to the training of lay magistrates, for instance, or the training of minor officials – consultants or counsellors, little ombudsmen, if you like – to help poor and semi-literate people deal with the ramifications of bureaucracy that too often govern their lives.

Work of this sort should command an adequate financial return. Its returns in terms of human happiness, human worth, and human stability, can be great and sociologically extremely significant. The need for it is there, but institutional thinking – the thinking, that is, of government, educators and the professions – has not yet come to grips with it.

There is also the vast and largely unexploited field of the true amateur – the man or woman who undertakes serious and important work for the love of it. It is unfortunate that we have in large degree come to equate the importance of work with the money paid for it. There is valuable work to be done by dedicated amateurs in nearly all fields – amateur naturalists and amateur astronomers, for instance, amateur botanists and amateur horticulturists, have all made major contributions in their fields and can make more. Such people are not mere hobbyists; they are much more than that. Working at some routine job to earn a living – perhaps in the not too distant future, simply living on a guaranteed annual income – they devote untrammeled and unspecialized minds to specialized fields because they choose to.

So far there has not been much time in North American civilization for the dedicated amateur. Until recently few people had sufficient leisure, and professionals on the whole have not been receptive. To some extent it is also true that sciences have become more complex and sophisticated. It is here that education can be of assistance, by providing courses that will give the amateur an understanding sufficient for his purpose without the many non-essentials that are considered necessary for the professional. There is, after all, a substantial difference. The professional wants and needs the stamp of professional approval on himself and his work; the amateur merely wants the means of getting at the meat of his subject in an interesting and useful way.

I see no reason why some form of "amateur training" cannot be developed in the course of ordinary education, so that an individual could go out into the world equipped, let us say, to operate heavy equipment – and at the same time sufficiently informed in some field of his choice to do good amateur work. Adult education courses are already directed somewhat towards this end, but obviously they can be carried much farther once a demand is established. Professional scientists should also become more aware of the potential of the gifted amateurs; in the field of environmental sciences alone there should be room for distinguished and valuable work by thousands of amateurs within the next few years.

You may feel that these tentative and speculative suggestions merely scratch the surface of the problem we are examining. They do exactly that and no more than that because, ultimately, the quality of living is an individual matter. Life is to be lived, not denied. It is quite short, full of contrasts and not without troubles and difficulties. Men have shown that life can be lived under the simplest circumstances with deep and satisfying meaning or under opulent circumstances in frustration and misery.

When we were young and inclined to be frivolous about our affairs, our elders would sometimes ask: "Do you want to spend your life digging ditches?" Since that time I have dug a few ditches, with considerable satisfaction and respect for the art. One can take pride in the straightness of a ditch, the slope of its sides, the accuracy of its incline. I have known at least one man of whom it was said in his community, with real respect: "He is a good man with a shovel." He had other distinctions, but I know he took pride in this one.

I am not recommending ditch-digging as a way of life. Anyway, machines now do the job and it is not unacceptable to be a good man with a backhoe. What I am suggesting is that there is more to most jobs than readily meets the eye and that satisfactions can be found in unlikely places.

The real human function is not simply to produce, or fill a job slot, or make money. It is to sharpen perceptions, physical and mental; to sharpen senses and sensitivity towards other human beings, towards the artificial world and the natural world; to grow and keep on growing from cradle to grave. This is not done without thought, effort, training, and selection. Senses are sharpened by using them, not by denying them; perception is sharpened by unclouded awareness, by contemplation and by renewed effort to perceive. Growth comes from learning—learning from life, from books, from people, from everything the senses can perceive.

The real quality of living is in the individual rather than in his surrounding conditions or even his opportunities. This is not to say that surroundings are unimportant or that opportunities cannot be improved. There is no age at which one cannot be shown some familiar thing in a way that makes it new and strange and wonderful—and continue thenceforth to see with a new degree of perception and a new level of joy. A sense of wonder is often considered the property of children; a sense of wonder retained or regained can be the stamp of maturity.

It is no longer enough – if it ever was – for educators to say: "Young man, or young woman, we have trained you in a trade, a vocation, a profession. Go forth, work steadily, and pay your taxes." By far the larger part of life is in other things, and it is the sum of these other things that makes for real quality in performance and in living. It is in responsiveness as much as in responsibility, in generosity more than in efficiency, in perceptiveness as well as in knowledge, in curiosity and wonder more than in acceptance and steadiness. It is in living rather than in serving out time. Schools cannot teach all of these things, but they can play a great part in opening the way into them.

19

Some Approaches to Conservation
(1966)

Any radical approach to conservation, to be successful, must include a radical redefinition of economic values, a radical shift in North American purpose, and radical redirection of the individual North American character. All three of these changes are already taking place, but slowly and gradually – so gradually that the loss and damage may be far beyond repair before they become fully effective.

North American economics, purpose, and character have all been directed to the opening up and development of a continent, at whatever cost to the future. Economic concepts have been short-term, wasteful, geared to maximum profit and further development. Purpose has been largely materialistic, the realization of wealth from resources. The ideal character has been ruthless, aggressive, pragmatic and self-centred – most clearly expressed by the concept that "nice guys don't win ball games" – or get rich or run successful companies or open up a continent.

All this was effective enough in its time and place. It did, in fact, open up a continent and it has realized enormous wealth from resources that were there for the taking. But it has persisted far beyond its time. Ideals that were useful in opening a continent are weak, childish, and unpleasant when applied to the task of making wise and satisfactory use of a continent already opened up.

The shift in thinking that can lead to living in harmony with the continent instead of battling it into destruction already exists, but it is so far undirected, inarticulate, shamefaced, and uncertain. Communities still struggle in ridiculous competition for growth through industrial development, blind to the fact that in so doing they welcome destruction of the very factors that made their living places desirable. Industrial companies are permitted to grow into monsters of wealth, with political power that rivals that of government itself. Rabbit-brained development schemes are sanctioned by government to support lame duck politicians. Government itself expends heedless billions in military destruction. Then, knowing all too little of the land it lives on and the seas that surround it, wastes hundreds of billions in a race to an empty and barren moon. The moon is there; like the summit of Everest it must someday be reached. But it is a matter for the co-operative effort of mankind, not for idiotic and immature competition.

None of these evils is necessary, none represents the ideals or desires or real interests of the young people of the United States and Canada. They are the yield of stale thinking that inflicts itself upon the young and stultifies the instinctive reach for a new way and new ideals. Any honest and coherent effort by government, industry, universities, and schools would advance this new way and these new ideals by a full generation, if not two. It would call only for understanding of the simple fact that land, air, and water must themselves be properly served by men.

Only ideas can achieve and only ideas of this kind can produce a radically new approach to conservation. Given any substantial measure of power I should first attempt to produce a North American man generous in spirit, in love with his environment, dedicated to its enhancement and preservation, secure in the knowledge that he can make it produce for all his needs and more besides. Given the shocking legacy of polluted waters, damaged lands, destroyed forests, shrinking wildlife, sectional jealousies, political intolerance, and racial hatred that youth today inherits, it should be no more difficult to develop a generous and conservation-minded man than it was to develop the ruthless and aggressive individual who fought the land to open the continent. The need for this new man is every bit as urgent and compelling as was the need for the other in his time.

The factors against him, of course, are massive. Cheap and cheaply bought politicians, big industry, Chambers of Commerce, "developers" and speculators of all kinds, uncontrolled government-created monsters such as the U.S. Army Engineers and, worst of all, the burden of outworn concepts and traditions. But the new North American man is developing in spite of them all. Nowhere is his development more apparent than in the immense public drive against pollution. Here time is fast running out, has almost run out already, and the dangers are apparent. The man is responding to the clear needs of his times and needs only the wise and determined backing of government at all levels to achieve the first and perhaps the most important triumph. Were I a man in power I should be a man in a hurry – in an awful hurry – to make full use of this new spirit and bring it to its triumph in the shortest possible time. Having done so, I should immediately call again upon the new North American man in his new-found strength and urge him to new ideas and new triumphs. He would have little difficulty in finding them.

The United States spends a fortune in foreign aid, too often with little effective result. Why then ruin river systems to make cheap power to suck bauxite away from underdeveloped nations so that the wages and profit of manufacture can be secured for Canada and the United States?

Why clutter the countryside with the yield of the packager's art and the waste of planned obsolescence? There is immense profit in both of these things. Why not a built-in tax on every bottle and tin can and piece of plastic, every automobile and washing machine and refrigerator, to take care of its ultimate disposal? True, such a tax might change substantially the arts of packaging and the planning of obsolescence, but that could only be gain.

Why are we arguing about the circumpolar abundance of the polar bear and the merits of the exhibitionists who hunt them for sport? Why don't we stop the hunting and find out about the abundance? And in the meanwhile, they aren't eating themselves out of house and home and no one needs to hunt them except the Eskimos.

Why can't we secure parks and wilderness areas and wild rivers and the other spectacular things of the continent hard and fast in the heart of the Constitution, so that they will be safe from violation even if the biggest goddammed diamond mine or oil well or underground facsimile of the whole General Motors complex is found in one of them? Why not? Has industry some inalienable right to invade public lands wherever found and destroy them?

The truth is that where land or water seems to be unclaimed, or weakly claimed, someone will try to claim them. Conservation must stake its claims, aggressively and authoritatively, ecologies are the key to the preservation of all forms of wildlife, including fish and plants. Ecologies must be recognized, assessed, understood, and defined; only then can they be adequately protected. Where wildlife populations are concerned, maximum seasonal ranges and requirements must be determined and fully protected. Management, which should be unobtrusive, and use, confirm such claims. Where populations and habitat are in balance, the "non-consumptive" use of naturalists, botanists, observers, camera enthusiasts, and others, should be paramount.

Pollution is the most serious threat to fisheries of all kinds, but since it is also a threat to every other water use there is real hope of abatement and prevention. After pollution, unneeded and ill-planned dams and diversions are the greatest

175

destroyers. A massive angling population has staked impressive claims to both fresh and saltwater areas, but is too little aware of the importance of preserving and improving ecological conditions as the prime means of ensuring adequate fish populations. In this field I admire the efforts of such organizations as Trout Unlimited, whose objective is "the preservation and improvement of wild trout waters." Improvement is a key word there. Such modern management methods as flow control, temperature control, gravel improvement, bank protection, can be highly constructive. When applied, they help to establish clear claims to the waters they serve. In many parts of the continent it is possible to enlist public interest and sympathy by providing attractive opportunities for the observation of spectacular movements or concentrations of fish populations, and this also can be of real assistance in establishing and maintaining claims.

20
Pollution for Profit
(1970)

Pollution is a pervading issue. It is no longer possible to consider any plan for the development or improvement of the self-reproducing natural resources without the qualification: "provided pollution can be controlled." One cannot really have any constructive thought for the betterment or even the continued existence of mankind without the same proviso, stated or unstated. No one seems to know for certain whether we have, as yet, passed the point of no return. But no intelligent person can doubt that if the present misuse of the so-called fossil fuels and assorted broad spectrum poisons continues much longer, there will have been created a whole range of irreversible ecological changes within which plant and animal life of any kind will be able to exist only by difficult and damaging feats of adaptation.

It is obvious that the only effective control of pollution on this scale must be by international agreement and performance. But this does not alter the fact that massive pollutions are no more than the sum of an infinity of minor pollutions. Each of these minor pollutions has its own local major effects. Whatever massive dangers there may be, the responsibility to detect, assess, and fight local pollutions remains as strong as ever, and the direct self-interest in doing so is in no way reduced.

Hunters, fishermen, naturalists, and other outdoor enthusiasts, were aware of the damaging effects of pollutions before most other groups. Yet even these natural observers are only now realizing how subtle, insidious, and ruinously cumulative the effects of pollution can be. While simple observation and direct attack on observed problems are just as important as they ever were, it is increasingly necessary to call upon, and support, provincial, national, and even international organizations.

DDT is an obvious villain among the unselective pesticides because it has been so widely and carelessly used. It is practically indestructible and therefore cumulative. It is collected into water courses everywhere and poured through the life-producing estuaries into the seas. It is collected again by small forms of life, passed through them to larger creatures and accumulated at each stage to the point at which some higher forms of wildlife are already threatened with extinction. Mankind has not escaped. Some scientists believe that the expected life span of North American man has already been significantly reduced by the quantities of DDT carried in his body.

If the use of DDT stopped everywhere in the world today, its effects would continue for at least another fifty years. The World Health Organization has recently decided that a total ban on the use of DDT is not yet possible because of the lack of suitable alternatives for the control of malaria and other sub-tropical diseases. Canada, clearly enough, has no such problem. DDT has been used extensively, particularly on the east coast, for spruce budworm control, with disastrous effect on other resources and highly debatable effects on the forests. Effective and somewhat less harmful alternatives are available. Surely there can be no possible case for further use of DDT in Canada. Michigan, Illinois, and other states, have already banned its use and the time for Canada to act on a nationwide basis is now, before further damage is done.

Getting rid of DDT will not solve the whole problem of chemical compounds used as insecticides, fungicides, and herbicides in agriculture and forestry. In the present state of knowledge at least some of them are essential. But new compounds are produced all the time and put into use with little or no knowledge of their real effects. Dieldrin, haptachlor, and chlordane, to name only three, are already found to excess in animal populations throughout the continent. The deadly effects of mercury compounds, used in industry, including pulp mills, as well as in agriculture, are only beginning to be checked and measured. This absurd situation, which leaves the world population secure in the knowledge that it is being daily poisoned, and wondering only in what degree, exists simply because the general onus in law is on the sufferer to prove that damage has been caused rather than upon the user to prove that no damage will result from his actions or "experiments." Anyone who has had any dealings with the law understands the difficulty of proving a negative, nevertheless the law requires this in much lesser matters than that of wholesale poisoning; if, for instance, you are found in impaired condition in the driver's seat of an automobile, you are required to prove that you "did not enter or mount the vehicle for the purpose of setting it in motion." Surely it is time now to insist that the producer or user of dangerous substances prove in advance that no damage will be caused.

Nearly all pollution can be defined as the use of a public asset (land, air, or water) for private profit (that is, the cheap disposal of unwanted wastes). Until very recently this has been an accepted, if not acceptable use, and the onus has always been on the long-suffering and largely unrepresented public to prove both the source and the degree of damage suffered. In fact, of course, the public should not be unrepre-

179

sented; it elects governments to protect its interests. But governments, for reasons respectable and otherwise, have been all too easily persuaded that pollutions, unless or until proved otherwise, are in the interests of the public.

This is an "extensive" resource use concept, applicable only in the course of developing relatively unsettled and unused areas and applicable then only at great cost to the future, as we are now painfully realizing. We are no longer struggling for a foothold upon a continent. We have made our devastating way across the continent and must now learn to live in peace and co-operation with it – that is, we are bound to turn to intensive, rather than extensive, use of resources; we must learn to live with the land and its creatures instead of against them, understand them instead of abusing them, love them instead of hating them. Governments, provincial governments especially, have not yet grown up to these ideas and a good proportion of the public is lulled and lagging with them.

In British Columbia, the ready acceptance of pollution as a way of life has been comprehensive and truly appalling. With a population of only two million we are already within sight of destroying or seriously damaging some of our finest assets, before we have had the time or the intelligence to put them to intensive use. The Fraser River, the Lower Fraser Valley, the Gulf of Georgia, the forests of Vancouver Island, Okanagan Lake, the Skeena River, the Fernie Valley are all under some form of visible threat. What are we doing about it? In my opinion, just about nothing. And we are not likely to do anything effective without some sharp change of thinking.

In British Columbia we are still thinking in terms of "How much pollution can we get by with?" This is exactly the wrong question. The question that must be asked and re-asked and asked again, times without end, is this: "How tightly can we control pollution?" It must be asked and answered and the answer must be acted upon in the case of every pollution that already exists and every pollution that is planned or projected, whether municipal, industrial, agricultural, or social, whether of air, land or water. We do not ask this question because we are still in the business of subsidizing industry, municipalities, and agriculture by allowing them to dispose of their wastes just about as they choose. The Minister of Health came close to setting up the question a year or so ago, when he proposed to announce pollution standards for the province. The Minister of Lands and Forests was prompt to cut him down. Standards will be announced, no doubt, at some future time – the Minister of Lands and Forests has promised them – but it is certain they will be designed to cause no inconvenience to industry, to municipal governments, to the provincial government or even the federal government. They will carefully reflect the wrong question, and they will be subject to easy revision should some miscalculation or political expediency direct them towards the right question.

The easy explanation for this perversion of rational behaviour is usually given in one word: economics. It is necessary then to ask: What economics? Whose economics? The economics of industry, real estate operators, and conservative government, or the economics of long-term public interest? They are by no means the same thing.

It is perfectly true that an all-out attack on pollution would cause some temporary reduction of the superficial standard of living. For most people the actual standard of living would be improved almost immediately by such items as clean air to breathe, clean food to eat, and clean waters in the streams, in the lakes, and along the beaches. There would be a cleanliness throughout the cities, along the highways, and wherever people go that would in itself be an enhancement of life. These are not small things; they are things that many people are starved for and dreaming of, but cannot have while their governments continue to fight rear-guard actions in defence of "profitable" pollution.

There would be other, more obviously material, possibly more significant gains. All pollution is waste. If wastes can be disposed of cheaply by dumping them into the nearest water (other people's water) or pouring them into the air (other people's air) or dumping them on the land (other people's land), then there is little or no incentive to convert waste to use. Municipalities pour out untreated or partially treated wastes that are rich in nutrients. The much-vaunted pulp mills waste from fifty to sixty-five per cent of the wood they use. All the internal combustion engines are grossly inefficient and wasteful – not because they have to be so but because that is the way we have been persuaded to want them.

At present society is carefully planned to encourage and reward waste of this type because it is "cheaper," more "productive," more "efficient." The words are not utterly perverted if one can maintain a special, half-blind viewpoint. Present methods are "cheap" – if one disregards the eventual cost of clean-up; a billion dollars to clean up New York's Hudson River, for instance, another billion and forty years of work to clean up Washington's Potomac. They are "productive," if one forgets that only the earth itself is productive and that its capacity is finite. They are "efficient," if one can disregard the wasted labour and dissipated resources that flow out with the effluents.

The Fraser watershed is the most impressive physical feature of British Columbia. It drains the richest half of the province. Its waters are put to an infinity of uses. It has built a magnificent delta on which nearly half the population of the province chooses to live. Its flood waters pass northward a hundred miles through the Gulf of Georgia to Cape Mudge, swing southward from there along the east coast of Vancouver Island to mingle with the turbulence of the tides, and reach the ocean through the Strait of Juan de Fuca. It also happens to be the greatest salmon producer in the world, in spite of past abuses, with a potential for much greater production.

For over a hundred years now the towns of the Lower Fraser Valley have been emptying their raw sewage into the river in ever-increasing quantities. It isn't really surprising that the beaches of the City of Vancouver and other nearby places are polluted. It isn't surprising that the salmon nets dredge up sludge and toilet paper. It isn't surprising that fisheries scientists are beginning to wonder how much longer the salmon runs can stand the stress of travelling through that debased and loathsome reach of water. It isn't surprising that informed people are wondering how long it will be before signs of damaging ecological changes will be detected in the Gulf of Georgia itself. What is altogether surprising is that the municipalities and the people who live in them have accepted this filthy performance for so long and seem fully prepared to go on adding to it.

The means of controlling municipal sewage have been known for a very long time. There is nothing difficult about them. Thousands of municipalities and cities have put them into effect. It costs money to do so, but it always costs more later; pollution costs, too, and more than money. Municipal pollution is fundamentally a provincial responsibility, but because provincial leadership has been so deficient and municipal responsibility has been so inadequate, it is now a national problem. The federal government can, and should, offer both leadership and a significant measure of subsidy. Federal standards should be high and specific. Subsidies should be calculated to enforce aggressive provincial co-operation and improvement beyond federal standards. Provincial governments should provide major subsidies, set close time limits, and penalize default. Within ten years every municipality in Canada should be providing primary and secondary treatment of wastes and looking for some constructive use of the remaining nitrates and phosphates. There are plenty of possibilities.

Municipalities are the greatest polluters and there is no excuse for them because they are us, you and me, offending ourselves and injuring our neighbours. But industrial polluters are not far behind them in quantity of pollution and sometimes ahead in quality because of the toxic nature of their effluents. There is much long established industrial pollution of the lower Fraser that is very inadequately controlled. Upriver pollution is comparatively new and consists so far mainly of pulp mill effluents. Minimum controls for fisheries purposes have been set by the Federal Department of Fisheries. But allowing pulp mills to discharge effluents into the river is like playing Russian roulette with the salmon runs, with every additional mill another loaded chamber. Breakdowns and miscalculations can and do occur. One Fraser mill has not yet, so far as I know, been able to meet the required standards and should have been closed long ago. One projected mill would be so poorly placed that a single breakdown would cause major damage, perhaps for a long period.

Pulp mills, whether situated on fresh or tidal waters, are an interesting problem in pollution because of the enormous quantity of their waste, its high proportion of solids and its chemical complexity. Forecasting effects has proved extremely difficult, especially in tidal waters, and standards were for a long time extremely lax. There is some indication of tightening standards, but we are far from applying the sort of pressures or inducements that would encourage intensive efforts to put the waste to use. Air pollution from pulp mills is usually considered in terms of its extremely unpleasant smell and its destructive effects on paintwork and other property. An even more important and interesting question is its effect on forest growth. Sulphur dioxide is well-known to be grossly inhibitive to plant growth, especially evergreens, and other sulphur compounds may be just as injurious. If the loss of annual growth on timberlands such as those of the Alberni Valley through air pollution from the mills were calculated, control at almost any cost might seem not merely economically sound but highly profitable.

Control of industrial pollutions, as of municipal pollutions, calls for strong federal leadership because provincial responsibilities have been so grossly neglected. Again, it should be a matter of generous inducements and sharp penalties. But federal leadership without whole-hearted provincial co-operation would be meaningless, and neither is likely to come about without the strongest public pressure, relentlessly maintained from election to election and firmly expressed in the polling booths on every election day, federal, provincial, or municipal.

Whether such pressure can be generated and maintained remains to be seen. It will not grow out of old-line thinking or old-line priorities. It will call for at least some temporary material sacrifice and a conscientious reassessment of values. It calls for informed leadership from universities and other learned institutions, as well as from dedicated groups of citizens such as the B.C. Wildlife Federation, SPEC and others. It calls for individual conviction and endless plain speaking. If the young people of the sixties have meant only a fraction of what they have said about creating a better world for living, the seventies may well see a major clean-up of the North American continent. In B.C. the problem is much smaller. Within a decade it should be possible to control all pollutions to rigid minimums and put most of the wastes to constructive use. It is an opportunity that will not last. With every year that passes the problem grows, the vested interests become more strongly entrenched, the cost of reversal grows greater. "Pollution for profit" is nineteenth-century thinking, but B.C. has plenty of nineteenth-century minds still around to support it. They are not easily put under. Unless the twentieth century takes over now, and with determination, many precious things will have been lost beyond recovery.

21
Crying in the Wilderness: Wildlife
(1953)

Many people besides hunters and naturalists are interested in wildlife. In plain fact, almost everyone is. The hunter needs a certain abundance of his chosen species, or he will not get much sport. The ordinary observer needs this abundance too, or he will not see very much. And the seeing of wild game, or of other wild creatures that are not classed as game, is a very real and intense pleasure; one has only to listen to the average tourist or camper or hiker's description of his last trip to know this. Nearly always the high spot will be the chance sighting of wild creatures in their natural surroundings.

My own views on the matter may be a little specialized, but I believe a chance to see wildlife under natural conditions is one of the important rights of man. It is a real enrichment of living. Believing this, I often feel that the right to hunt and kill game is far more questionable than the right simply to see it and watch it for the pleasure of seeing and watching, and perhaps learning a little. But my conviction on this point is far outweighed by the realization that hunters are almost the only effective protectors of wildlife. Without their interest, without their strong organization and overwhelming conviction that they have a stake in the natural order of things, game and wildlife would disappear before the advance of civilization far more rapidly than it does; and this is true of old countries as well as new ones.

The interests of the hunter and the observer of wildlife are rarely at odds. In the old days of market-hunting the hunter could and did kill off whole species, or reduce them to rarity. Today he can be checked in this long before the danger point is reached, and very often he acts as a useful control on game species that would become a nuisance to farming and other interests, and so might be wiped out as pests. He is a control also upon species, such as deer, that would otherwise exhaust the yield of their feeding ranges and so pass into eclipse after temporary abundance. And the hunter spends money, in licences and gear and travel, which justifies the expenditure of government funds to protect the creatures that interest him.

To understand modern ideas of wildlife management, it is essential to realize that the emphasis has shifted from protecting breeding stocks to the protection and improvement of feeding and living areas. A very small number of animals under ideal breeding and feeding conditions can rapidly increase to a very large number; under bad conditions the finest breeding stock in the world will just as rapidly drop off to a very small number. In most parts of Canada wildlife populations are controlled by the extent and quality of winter feeding areas available to them. You may, for instance, have a valley whose slopes and mountain meadows are capable of feeding a herd of several thousand elk and deer through the summer; but if the animals are forced down by winter snows to a few acres of the valley floor, as they always are, that valley will support only two or three hundred elk, not several thousand. If you spread settlement over those wintering acres, or drown them under water behind a power dam, then the herd will be wiped out altogether.

Many people believe that the great areas of virgin forest supported enormous quantities of wildlife, and that what we have left is a pale shadow of former abundance. This is not so at all. Heavy timber is not good game-producing land; the trees block out the sunlight and take up all the good for themselves. I have travelled for days and weeks through virgin stands of Douglas fir and hemlock and cedar and seen nothing but squirrels and a few birds; the game was in the open places, in the swamps and alder flats, along the stream edges and up on the bluffs and ridges. As soon as the heavy timber is cut away and shrubs and plants and young deciduous trees have a chance to grow, wildlife multiplies to abundance. This is the source of the present abundance of deer and blue grouse on Vancouver Island, and in so many of the coast forest areas that have been logged over.

Even in the logged areas, winter range for wildlife is limited, far less than enough to support the natural increase of population through a winter of deep snow. So, the biologists tell us, the hunter not only prevents waste of deer that would have died off anyway during the winter; he also gives the survivors a chance to come through in good shape and produce a maximum crop of healthy fawns the following spring. Since a weak, half-starved doe may lose her fawns or produce only one fawn instead of healthy twins, it can be shown that the herd may be improved in both quality and numbers by heavy cropping in the hunting season.

Like deer, blue grouse increase enormously as the country is opened up by logging. In heavy forest they are a comparatively scarce bird, but current research suggests they are extremely hardy and well adapted to winters of heavy snow; something like seventy per cent of them survive each year and the average blue grouse has a life expectancy of four years – an almost unheard of figure for game birds. Since great numbers also go back each year from the hunting areas into the high hills before the first shot of the season is fired, it would seem that they should increase to the proportions of a plague. The reason they do not is that after the first three or four years of rapid increase on clean ground, certain parasites take over. Practically every chick is infested within its first two weeks of life and at five weeks the broods have dropped off to an average of rather less than two; just enough to maintain the population at a constant level until some new factor, such as the regrowth of the timber, comes in to change the balances again.

The blue grouse and deer of the slash areas are a good instance of one industry, logging, that may increase wildlife populations. Beaver, elk, bear, band-tail pigeons, and many small birds, are pretty certain to increase in logged-over areas also, and the beaver ponds tend to encourage populations of nesting ducks and other swamp-loving creatures. But the increase is a temporary one, very rapid and noticeable for the first ten or twenty years after logging, then gradually levelling off as the trees take over the ground again. Tremendous areas of this land are being held by the province or by private companies for the regrowth of the timber to useful size, which takes about a hundred years. The advantage of keeping them open and as fully accessible as possible to tourists, hunters, and ordinary citizens, during the regrowth period is obvious – it means that a hundred annual crops of sport and recreation can be taken from the land while one timber crop is maturing. The most serious problem in realizing this double yield is fire. But tight closures during periods of extreme hazard, and the sort of co-operation that can be expected from an educated public should keep the risk within bounds. Extensive use of the woods is a measure of protection in itself, since it ensures early detection of fires and can help to pay for adequate patrolling.

Farm land, like logging slash, produces far more wildlife than forest land, and presumably will always do so since it is axiomatic that the richer the land is, the more abundant and varied will be the wildlife on it. Deadly sprays used on some crops may be a threat to the future, though their use is less fashionable than it was. But the farmer is a far more intensive crop-grower than the forester and his crops are far more sensitive to abuse, whether this be the depredations of wildlife or the plain misconduct of the hunter or visitor. For this reason the public will never be able to claim right of access to farm land as it can to forest land. It will have to depend instead, as it has in the past, on the good will of the farmer and its own reputation for decent behaviour.

Less than five per cent of British Columbia's area is farm land. The rest is forest and mountain and grazing land, land that seems likely to remain forever in a more or less primitive state, and which should remain in public hands. This sounds like an encouraging picture, but unfortunately most forms of wildlife need a share in the lowlands of the province, the flat, productive valley floors, for their survival. Industrial and agricultural developments and increasing settlement will always be a threat and there is not much doubt that B.C. will lose valuable wildlife areas from time to time. The point is to protect those that can be protected and to compensate as far as possible for the lost areas.

The record since the war has not been too encouraging. Important wildlife wintering areas in Tweedsmuir Park will be destroyed by flooding behind the Nechako dam, and so far as I know this point was not even discussed in planning the development. In Strathcona Park, the B.C. Power Commission's dam will destroy the last remaining natural sample of Pacific Coast wildlife conditions, and will either wipe out or displace the last elk herd still living the year around in primitive forest. At least these points were brought out into the open, but they represent irreplaceable losses, for which future generations will most properly blame us.

On the whole we have done better with the breeding and nesting grounds of wildfowl than with more general wildlife areas, perhaps because of the years of mistakes in the prairie provinces. Sportsmen and naturalists were able to save a good part of the famous Duck Lake in the Kootenay country from drainage for agricultural purposes. Millions of dollars have been and are being spent on the prairies to restore

190

marshes – wastefully drained in misguided attempts to create farmland – and it would be too bad if we had to repeat this folly in the far more limited breeding areas of B.C. Victoria sportsmen successfully prevented Sidney Lagoon, an important feeding and resting place for wildfowl, from becoming a booming ground. Best of all, the B.C. game department secured the reservation of a large area on Tofino Inlet as a wildfowl sanctuary and public shooting ground. Tofino Inlet is the most important single resting place for migrating ducks and geese on the Pacific flyway, but when the reservation was first suggested the Minister of Lands of that time objected that the area might "someday be needed for booming logs or growing oysters." Fortunately the objection was overruled, but it typifies the sort of thinking that any far-sighted effort to preserve wildlife runs into.

One of the difficulties of protecting wildlife resources is that their destruction is a creeping, cumulative thing. A nesting area is destroyed by drainage here, a feeding area becomes a mill or factory site, a wintering ground is drowned behind a power dam, or exhausted by encroaching cattle; so-called sportsmen, or thoughtless small boys with twenty-twos, shoot off bald eagles and ospreys and the many beneficial hawks; others fail to recover their wounded game, and shoot more; still others kill game, black bears, perhaps, or mergansers or fish-eating mallards, that they have no intention of recovering. All these things add up to loss and destruction. Legislation can help sometimes – it might, for instance, give the bald eagle a chance to survive in settled areas, instead of being wiped out as it has been in the State of Washington. But the most serious losses are often caused by short-term industrial expediency. Only an informed public with a lively conscience can prevent them.

22

Some Thoughts of Paradise
(1972)

British Columbia has an abundance of lakes, rivers, streams, and creeks, fed by high rainfall, winter snows, and the glaciers of the big mountains. It has an inland sea, thousands of miles of protected coastline with deep inlets, narrow passages, and many islands. The waters produce and foster five species of salmon, two native trouts, each with sea-running variants, char, whitefish, grayling, and other cold-water fishes.

In its wild state, this adds up to a sports fisherman's paradise and, indeed, the province has been just that and still is in substantial degree. But many sins and errors have crept into paradise over the past hundred years and especially during the past thirty or forty years. Paradise is by no means all that it was, yet thousands more fishermen come to it every year in search of yesterday's dream. Can the dream be realized? Can paradise be reclaimed?

I believe the answer to both questions is "Yes." Fishermen's dreams, of course, are notoriously extravagant and not all will be realized to the full. Paradise regained will never be an exact copy, but it will have its compensations and may even exceed the original in some respects. But it can be regained only by taking thought, by reaching deep understanding of its nature and by working to restore it according to its nature.

The province's major game fisheries fall into three divisions: the saltwater fishery, mainly for salmon; the trout fishery of the interior lakes; and the fisheries of the coastal streams and lakes, where cutthroats are preponderant but the steelhead runs are the chief attraction.

The saltwater fishery and the salmon runs are a federal responsibility and it is just as well they are; had they been left to provincial neglect and rapacity, there might be little remaining of them today. The saltwater fishery has always benefitted indirectly from the research, management, and protection of the commercial species, and it is now benefitting directly by much closer attention to the most important game species, the chinook and the coho. Over the past several years, it has become increasingly evident that fish which live most of their lives in inside waters, especially the Strait of Georgia, make up the bulk of the sports catch. Careful management has brought about a significant recovery of the chinook salmon and this is likely to continue, especially if estuarial and saltwater nursery areas are protected. Coho stocks have also benefitted, though their recovery is less evident because of their dependence on a full year of stream life before migrating to the estuaries and salt water. Most chinooks spend only ninety days in the streams before moving out.

The degradation of stream conditions throughout the province is almost certainly the greatest single factor in the decline of salmon and steelhead runs, and this reflects a colossal failure in land management, especially forest land management. Chums, pinks, and sockeyes are least affected, the first two because they migrate to sea very soon after hatching, the sockeyes because they spend their freshwater rearing time in lakes. The coho, a frequenter of small streams, is greatly affected by low summer flows and high temperatures during its stream year, as well as by loss of terrestrial feed from forest overhang and damage to aquatic life by blocked and silted gravels. The steelhead is similarly affected, and losses of premigrants may be even greater since most B.C. steelhead spend two or three years in the streams before going out to sea.

The easy remedy for all this, the patent medicine panacea, is the hatchery with artificial rearing facilities. Hatcheries and hatchery techniques have a place – for research purposes, perhaps for building a run back to the point where it can take off, certainly for the stocking of interior lakes with resident species. But they have no place in maintaining anadromous fish stocks at high level over an indefinite period.

The weaknesses and limitations of hatcheries are by no means fully known as yet, but even in the present state of knowledge it is impossible to name a critical number. First of all, and most important, hatchery selection of spawners in time produces a highly specialized breed. The natural versatility of the stock, which is the best protection it can possibly have against disaster of all kinds, from disease to stream blockages such as the Babine slide of 1952, is utterly lost. Hatchery stocks can, in time, become incapable of spawning naturally. Hatchery and rearing procedures inevitably throw out the timing of the runs. Hatcheries, to be economic, must select from some narrow time range of return and this will be imprinted on the progeny.

Artificial rearing, to be reasonably economic, must produce migrant smolts in the shortest possible time. In terms of steelhead production, this means that the two- and three-year old smolts that B.C. rivers now produce must be grown to smolt size in one year – by no means an easy matter in the low winter temperatures normally prevailing in B.C. streams. This timing in all probability will affect the timing of the return – one-year smolts commonly return at small size after one year in the sea. Timing of return can be somewhat similarly affected in cohos.

Hatchery stocks can degrade wild stocks by inter-breeding

with them, thus reducing their range of variability and versatility and so their natural hardihood. It is said that in the State of Washington few uncontaminated wild steelhead stocks still exist; if so, it is not hard to assume that in time there will be no wild stocks at all and the continuation of the steelhead species will depend entirely on hatcheries. It is a discouraging prospect.

Finally, hatcheries are extremely costly, both in capital and in operation. A figure commonly given for hatchery steelhead returned to the angler's catch is around six to eight dollars apiece, and even this is probably a low estimate. At least one U.S. hatchery represents a capital investment of ten million dollars – and not at today's prices. B.C.'s Capilano hatchery is a capital investment of about five million dollars and any future hatcheries are unlikely to be cheaper. It is interesting to compare this to the International Salmon Commission's spawning channel program on the Fraser, which is expected to double the production of sockeye and pink salmon in the next sixteen years at a cost of only fourteen million dollars at 1971 values. While the comparison is not strictly a fair one because of the difference in freshwater rearing requirements of the species involved, it does suggest that hatcheries are a very costly venture, in addition to their other disabilities.

The best way of restoring salmon and steelhead runs to their full glory is the hard way: close protection and management of existing stocks, stream rehabilitation and improvement and greatly improved land management. In the long term there is, I believe, no other way than this.

One of the first essentials in coho salmon management is to determine which streams contribute mainly to the Strait of Georgia resident coho stocks. The obvious way to go about this is by a massive tagging of cohos during their final year in the Strait. The problem is tag recovery. It would be extremely difficult and costly to cover all the creeks and streams to which the tagged fish might return. One solution, I believe, would be to have every school in the areas adjacent to the Strait of Georgia "adopt" a creek or section of stream and become thoroughly familiar with all its features and characteristics in advance of the tagging program. This could and should be done as part of the school curriculum, as it could and should have extremely significant educational effects. The tagging program could be commenced one or two seasons after the start of this "familiarization" stage and significant tag recoveries would be ensured.

Once the main producing streams of the Strait of Georgia stocks are known, it would be easy to justify substantial expenditures in improvement and development work. There are still other ways of attacking the problem – for instance, by marking pre-migrant fry or smolts in the more likely streams – but I believe the program I have suggested above, provided it is adequately organized and led, is the most promising one.

Fisheries authorities are inclined to object that we do not understand stream rehabilitation or stream improvement sufficiently well to spend important money on it. The answer to that is: the sooner we learn about it the better, and the best way to learn about it is by doing. There are thousands of streams in B.C. that have been damaged by logging, fires, road building, mining operations, and other ill-managed land uses. Along hundreds of these, scars have healed, vegetation has grown back, disturbed earth has settled; yet damage remains in the streams themselves, in the shape of silted gravels, changed stream-bed conformation, unnecessary debris, and reduced productivity. We do know something of the results that can come from clean gravels, and some promising gravel-cleaning machinery and techniques have been developed. We know something of the benefits of controlled or partly controlled flows. We know the type of gravels that can restore depleted stream gravels, and where to find them. We know at least something of good stream conformation. We know, in fact, a great deal; it is true that we do not yet know how to get the most valuable effects from the least expenditure, but we will never find out until we start doing something.

We can also improve land use practices out of all knowledge. At present we are beset by unresolved conflicts between provincial and federal legislation – in the main between federal fisheries and provincial forestry. There is, at best, a little uneasy and inadequately informed co-operation. We accept, for instance, that it is a "good idea" to keep logging out of streams and protect stream-side vegetation. In practice, very little comes of it.

Provincial land use practice pays lip-service to the principle of "multiple use with priorities." Enormous tracts of land throughout the province, and especially on the coast, are committed to logging and forestry, the latter of a primitive sort, and through the whole of these areas the absolute priority is logging; pious references are sometimes made to multiple use, to consideration for recreation, for wildlife, for fisheries; and that is about as far as it goes.

This is no way to run a country, for the present or the future, but we are not likely to change it over night. But we can make a start. The start I propose is this: in all land within six hundred feet of any stream or lake the priority land uses should be fisheries and recreation, with forestry a secondary use where it is considered desirable. Administration of these lands should be in the absolute control of fisheries and recreational authorities.

This would not solve all the problems and it would certainly create some new ones, not least among them the recruitment and training of competent personnel. But, given this rearrangement of jurisdiction, co-operation would begin to mean something and multiple use would mean something. The time to get started on it is now, and "now" is a good fifty years later than it should have been.

With few exceptions, the basic stocks of fish – that is, the individual races of all species that have adapted to the specific local conditions of various waters – still exist. Given satisfactory conditions, they can renew their original abundance. In some instances they can be encouraged by artificial aids – spawning channels, flow control, temperature control, gravel improvement, and the removal of obstructions – to increase the original abundance or at least to maintain it with greater regularity over successive seasons.

One probable limiting factor in production is the rearing capacity of estuaries. We have been extremely careless about our river and stream estuaries, often sacrificing them without question to convenient industrial uses. We should be intensely concerned about estuary protection and it is probably time also to start to examine ways of extending, improving, and supplementing estuary capacities. It is not at all difficult to imagine ways in which this might be done, though a good deal of experimentation and research is necessary.

No conceivable system of hatcheries could ever produce more than a fraction of the results we can expect from natural restoration, and the cost of even a partial attempt would be prohibitive. Natural restoration, though far less costly and to a far greater extent self-sustaining, will still cost a good deal of money, and sports fishermen should be prepared to face this. The saltwater sports fisherman has always been something of a freeloader, paying no licence fee, depending on the bounty of federal expenditures for the commercial fishery. He now needs, and demands, expenditures specifically for the protection, management, and improvement of the sports fishery. He should be prepared to pay for them if he values the future of his sport. The saltwater resident licence fee should not be a mere token of a dollar or so a year, but something not less than ten dollars. Non-resident fees should be in proportion. We still have what might be called an exportable surplus of recreational fishery; but it is decreasing yearly, while the demand is increasing.

In addition to contributing at least something to the maintenance of his sport, the fisherman needs to direct his attention far more closely to the qualities that make it a sport. He should be more aware of his fish and their needs and so be ready to protect them. He should examine his sport closely and seek ways of refining it to give him greater pleasure – catching fourteen-inch grilse on a flasher and several ounces of lead, for instance, has nothing to do with sport and can scarcely afford much pleasure. The saltwater fisherman might do well to question whether it is in his interest to take these small fish at all or whether he would do better to let them grow larger. Some fishermen complain about having to return small fish and like to argue that most will not live. If handled with reasonable care they will live. And any fisherman who finds himself in a place where he is consistently hooking undersized fish, should get out of there and try somewhere else.

The steelhead fisherman should be very much concerned to protect his downstream smolts. These little fish are easily recognizable and they are very valuable – the larger, the more valuable, because size is an important factor in survival. I have seen Vancouver Island smolts as large as eleven inches long and believe that a fourteen-inch size limit is needed to protect them. Bait fishing at the time when smolts are migrating, even by children, is highly undesirable because it inevitably produces higher mortality than lure-fishing or flyfishing.

Both steelhead and salmon fishermen should give serious consideration to the pleasures – and they are very real pleasures – of catch-and-release fishing. It is reasonable enough to take half-a-dozen or even a dozen sizeable fish a season for the freezer, but few people can want more than that. There is no pleasure in knocking a fish on the head. There is a very real pleasure in carefully unhooking him, preferably while he is still in the water, gently nursing his strength back if necessary, then watching him swim away. If the job is well done he will recover completely. A fish can be hooked and released several times in a season by different fishermen and still go up his river to spawn in due time.

Catch-and-release is of particular importance to steelhead fishermen. Quite a number of steelheaders release all, or nearly all, their fish now and if the practice becomes more general one will be reasonably assured of good numbers of fish holding over in the pools throughout the season.

I have emphasized saltwater fishing and anadromous fish, because it is with these that the most work has to be done. I am convinced that all the salmon runs are important to sports fishermen, not only because both pink salmon and sockeyes are likely to appear in larger numbers in the catch as recovery goes on, but because the fertility and general productivity of our streams is closely related to abundant salmon runs. Big runs of spawning fish scour the silt out of the gravels and maintain a life-giving flow of water through them. Carcasses of the dead fish and waste eggs make food for aquatic life of all kinds. Emerging alevins and abundant free-swimming fry add to the food resources of the streams and estuaries.

The trout waters of the interior of the province present far fewer management problems, but good production and good fishing still call for close and careful management. Hatcheries have a part to play in this, because there are always new lakes to be stocked and those with limited or non-existent spawning areas must be constantly restocked. But it still important to examine the resource with care and, where possible, to develop and maintain self-reproducing stocks. Control of the fishery to maintain quality is critically important, and not the least important part of this will be in the control of outboard motor use. Motors are unnecessary on lakes of one thousand acres or less; nine- or ten-horsepower motors should be adequate on lakes up to four thousand acres, and I suspect this is too generous. Lakes above four or five thousand acres can probably stand larger motors, though their use should be prohibited near shoals, in bays, and other productive waters.

Gear restriction is an interesting question. "Fly-only" lakes are certainly an attractive and encouraging feature and should work no hardship on anyone, as a trolled fly is usually at least as effective as a cast fly. But in deep lakes with high summer surface temperatures some hardware fishing at greater depths may be desirable to keep stocks in balance. Size limits and catch limits should be closely calculated to the management requirements of individual lakes. The Kamloops trout is a superb animal and most of the interior lakes are highly productive. It should be possible to develop and maintain the finest lake trout fishing in the world, but this will not happen by itself.

Paradise can never be regained but, after all, Adam and Eve couldn't make full use of it until after the fall, and then it was too late. There is hope in the fruit of the Tree of Knowledge and hope in the honest sweat of the face. The secrets of the Tree of Life are gradually becoming known to us. We know that dams and pollution are destroyers of life. We know that the heritage of the natural fish stocks is self-perpetuating so long as they and their habitat are maintained. There is no need, then, to bewail lost innocence. We need only take knowledge and put it to work.

23

Our Ocean
Garbage Dump and Cesspool
(1972)

A recent press release suggested that a fifty-million-dollar copper smelter may be built in the Cariboo between Clinton and 70 Mile House. As part of the smelting process, some 350 to 375 tons of sulphur in sulphur dioxide would be discharged into the atmosphere every day. (Sulphur dioxide is a colourless gas with a gagging odour, which can be deadly to both vegetation and public health.) Even though there are pollution control devices which can contain most of the poisonous fumes, the companies concerned felt that installing full pollution-control equipment would not be economic. They also felt that tall stack "atmospheric emission of sulphur dioxide waste" would not cause "immediate or extensive harm" to the environment. While this method of control and dispersal seems akin to dumping garbage over a neighbour's fence, the companies concerned didn't feel that it was.

I wonder. Some 350 tons a day is over 127,000 tons of poisonous material a year – and what goes up is going to come down somewhere. To the east, in the probable set of the atmospheric drift, is a good section of B.C., then the prairie provinces and the rest of Canada.

It seems reasonable to consider these areas neighbourly.

To the west is the Pacific Ocean, British Columbia's fluid front yard. The Pacific, in common with all the world's oceans, just doesn't need any more industrial fall-out, sulphur dioxide or otherwise.

In fact, it can be said flatly that the risk and possibility of degrading the oceans and largely destroying their present and potential values is very real indeed. Without some change in present trends, I believe degradation and, ultimately, destruction of vital qualities is inevitable.

There is already broad-scale pollution through fall-out – of pesticides, nuclear wastes and industrial wastes. These are in addition to the inflow of similar wastes from the land. They are in addition to the deliberate dumping of oil, accidental spills of oil, and shipwreck. We have had clear warning of the world-wide effects of the chlorinated hydrocarbons, DDT and others, through damage to such bird species as pelicans, penguins, and arctic terns. Is it reasonable to suppose that fish, planktons, and ocean plant life are immune to similar effects?

These points alone seem adequate warning that the dilution capacity of the oceans is not inexhaustible. There are other clear warnings in the present state of enclosed seas such as the Mediterranean, the Baltic, the Black Sea, and others, where the effects of pollution are obvious. Salt water has no mysterious powers of absorption and elimination. Rather the opposite. The world's gulfs and seas and oceans are in fact all one single body of water in constant circulation. True, the rates of circulation may vary, but there is oxygen at the bottom of the deepest ocean trenches, constantly renewed by circulation; even over such a brief period of time as six years the bottom of the Tonga trench showed a significant temperature variation; again, clear evidence of circulation. This means that long-lived pollutants, such as pesticides and radioactive substances, can be dispersed over thousands of miles and eventually through the whole system of the oceans.

This is enough to suggest some of the threats to ocean productivity, past, present, and continuing. There is an increasing threat in the ocean transportation of oil by larger and larger tankers. There is a new threat in the possibility of deep-sea mining – the recovery of deposited minerals from the ocean bed; some scientists have suggested that major disturbance of bottom sediments (diatom or globigerina ooze covers about one-third of the ocean floor) may increase turbidity through large areas, reducing light penetration, and so the basic productivity of photosynthesis. The only real answer to such formidable questions as these is in international research and international co-operation and control far beyond anything that has yet been achieved. Perhaps the recent United Nations Conference on the Human Environment at Stockholm and the Law of the Sea Conference next year may produce better guidelines and regulation. But there will be oil money, mining money, chemical money, and military money still working steadily behind government scenes to frustrate any really significant progress – or even significant restraints.

Mankind has used the ocean as a garbage dump and cesspool for thousands of years. But there were far fewer men, producing far less sewage and garbage, and what was produced was chiefly organic and readily degradable. They were mainly substances occurring in nature and capable of natural assimilation. Even so, there were pollutions. Today, the works of men in shifting soil, destroying forests, dredging harbours, building dams, and similar activities, are of an entirely different order of magnitude; and the products of man are often compounds unknown to nature or massive yields from deep in the earth of substances that occur only in sparse or scattered form in surface waters. What is happening today in the rivers, in the river estuaries and lagoons and saltmarshes, in the shallow seas and out over the continental shelf, is a compound of these factors. This is the sensitive, highly productive perimeter of the oceans, and it requires no effort of the imagination to understand that it has already been gravely damaged in many areas or that its general degradation at an ever increasing rate will have widespread effects on the productivity of the ocean as a whole.

River estuaries, where fresh and salt water meet and tidal effects trap nutrients, are the most productive areas on the face of the earth. They are also the most used and most abused areas. We know far too little about estuaries, the complex secrets of their productivity or the mechanics of their protection, and we have left ourselves far too little time to find out. What we do know, or should know, is that their protection may well be critical to the survival of the human race.

I should like to consider very briefly one major Canadian estuary – the Fraser. The Fraser is one of the world's greatest salmon producers and at the same time significantly influences the productivity of the Strait of Georgia and the Strait of Juan de Fuca – conceivably also the west coast of Vancouver Island. We have dredged it and modified it, we pour into it thousands of tons of industrial and agricultural wastes and the municipal wastes, largely untreated, of more than a million people. We have, with ridiculous unconcern, planted the Roberts Bank Superport practically on top of it. There are a hundred schemes for other uses and modifications and we have even given serious consideration to one project (the Moran Dam) that would in due time erode the estuary out of existence.

Aesthetically, the Lower Fraser is already a filthy river. Fishermen haul toilet paper and human feces in their nets and wear rubber gloves to avoid infection. Yet by international standards the river is still relatively clean, kept so by its massive flow, and so far as we know salmon and other anadromous species still make safe passage through it, upstream and down. We now propose to add to all the other abuses a daily load of 129 million gallons of chlorinated sewage. Whether the river, the salmon or the estuary with all its varied production can stand this, no one really knows. That they cannot stand it without impairment, which would certainly be cumulative in the estuary itself, is obvious. It is obvious, too, that there are practiceable alternatives.

What is happening on the Fraser estuary has already happened in a hundred estuaries on the east side of the continent and dozens on the west side. Proposed river diversions into the canal system of California and Texas will destroy still more, as will dredging, land fill, and pollution.

The productive influences of natural river flows do not end in their estuaries. A major river in freshet will have a plume of fertility reaching a hundred miles or more beyond its mouth. Its silts and sands stabilize beaches and build productive flats. The freshwater input of the North Pacific is so great that salinity levels of the whole ocean north of 40° range below thirty-five parts per thousand, and at least one oceanographer has suggested that it might be considered a giant estuary. One might add the speculation that some of the fluctuations in ocean survival of sockeye, coho, and other anadromous stocks may well be related to it.

I hope I have said enough about estuaries to make their importance to ocean productivity clear and to emphasize the incredible abuses we subject them to. They are the richest source of life on the planet, quite possibly the critical source; and they are the least considered. Estuaries are also resilient; they can be restored and if we know what is good for us, I suspect that many will be over the next fifty years.

The Thames estuary, for instance, has been polluted for over one hundred years, yet during the past ten years, has undergone amazing rehabilitation. A recent issue of *Wildlife Review,* an excellent publication from the B.C. Department of Recreation and Conservation, contained the following information on this much abused waterway: "Tests made of the historic Thames River in 1957 revealed that there was practically no oxygen for a period of nine months along a forty-five-mile stretch of the waterway. No fish were present except eels.

"At a later date sewage plants were redesigned, other antipollution campaigns were launched, and effluent levels in the river were reduced dramatically. Today there are over fifty-five species of fish known to be present in the same forty-five-mile stretch of the Thames that was almost lifeless in 1957."

While international guidance and standards are needed, I believe that coastal states must always be the best guardians of coastal waters and their freshwater inflows. For this reason, as well as for many others, I believe that jurisdiction over coastal waters in regard to both fisheries and pollution should be greatly extended. Some fifteen nations already claim fisheries jurisdiction for one hundred miles or more off shore; more than fifty claim twelve-mile jurisdiction and a dozen claim jurisdiction in excess of three miles. Logically, jurisdiction should extend off shore at least to the start of the abyssal slope and responsibility for both water quality and the management and maintenance of fish stocks should rest with the coastal state.

The subtle nature of many onshore pollutions is worth noting. The destruction of California kelp beds, for instance, was only indirectly the result of Los Angeles sewage. This sewage fertilized plant life on the sea floor, sea urchins throve on the increased plant life, overpopulated the area and chewed away the kelp holdfasts in search for sustenance, producing a significant environmental change. Pollution is normally considered to be the addition of some toxic or injurious substance, but there can be similar effects by subtraction. If a river's natural silt burden is significantly reduced, for instance, predator-prey relationships in the estuary and well beyond it will be modified by improved visibility. Eel grass beds and other productive areas nearby will be modified, if not destroyed. Vertical distribution of plankton will be affected and species composition almost certainly modified. Any one of these changes is significant; taken together they could well be critical to a number of important fish stocks.

As the example of the Thames River indicates, all pollution can be controlled and that in the interest of society it

207

should be controlled, if not eliminated. In the past most industries and most municipalities have assumed a privilege, almost a divine right, to pollute. The attitude has been that drainage systems and rivers are there for the cheap and convenient disposal of effluents and no one should stand in the way of such economy and convenience. This attitude dies hard, but die it must. No waters, least of all fresh waters, should be used for the assimilation of wastes. The most that should be expected of them is that their assimilative capacity should provide a safety factor to take care of minimal residuals and the accidents that inevitably result from defective equipment or plainly human incompetence.

Ideally, pollution control begins at the very earliest stages of plant planning, and fisheries biologists as well as sanitation engineers and hydrologists have a place at that stage. Plant siting can be critical – proper consideration for environmental factors, for instance, would have immediately ruled out the totally inept siting of the Cherry Point oil refinery, with its fantastic hazards to the Strait of Juan de Fuca, Puget Sound, and the Strait of Georgia. For that matter, it could and should still be ruled out as a receiver of oceangoing tankers.

Properly informed and guided plant planning ensures effluent control at minimum cost and at levels of efficiency that can only be imposed later with great difficulty. All the pulp mills presently operating on the Fraser system were planned and built under this sort of control, and perhaps it is not altogether surprising that a Canadian investigating team found them superior in effluent disposal to any other mills in Canada, Europe or Scandinavia, and superior to all except one or two in the United States.

Even with these standards there will still be operating errors and inefficiencies which must be promptly detected and corrected. This calls for understanding and constant co-operation on both sides and genuine interest on the part of all employees. The latter is by no means an impossibility at today's levels of education and concern, though it must be achieved by fact and good relations rather than by simple authoritarianism.

These upriver mills on the Fraser are controlled to considerably higher standards than most mills on tidal water – a point of considerable interest, since it reveals that economics are not a major factor in proper effluent control. The tidal mills, which do cause environmental damage and fisheries losses, have the significant advantages of superior timber, deep water access and proximity to markets, so there is no reasonable doubt that they could be held to much higher standards than they have been.

It is important to remember that even with ideal legislation, sound planning and wise control, there will still be pollutions, some of them potentially disastrous, from energy and mining and agricultural activities, from oil and chemical transportation, from manufacturing and from the ordinary wear and tear of excessively concentrated human populations. This is why it is essential to minimize so-called allowable pollutions. The only protection against accidents and inefficiencies is in constant vigilance backed by prompt remedial action – action unrestricted by bureaucratic delays and fumblings. The co-operation of an informed public – the man on the job, outdoorsmen of all types, the ordinary citizen observer – is essential to success and it is vitally important to encourage and accept public participation in every possible way.

It goes without saying that the fishing industry itself must be above reproach in matters of pollution or waste. There is undoubtedly room for improvement, not only in the control of effluents, but in the utilization of wastes. There is room also for a greater effort, both by the industry itself and by individual fishermen who work in it, to enlist and inform public support. The present is a favourable time for this. The public is aware, as never before, of the losses and hazards of pollution. It is aware of the need for fisheries development and some of the possibilities of development. Without encour-

209

agement and a steady flow of sound information, it may not remain so. I suggest the full responsibility for building public interest in the resource should not rest with government but with all who use the resource or benefit from it.

In the last analysis, protection of the oceans is the vital concern of every man, woman and child on the face of the planet. The oceans are destructible, and the processes of degradation are already in operation – through oil spills, metallic and other inorganic wastes of many kinds directly introduced, through excess of organic wastes and through damage to estuaries; all this is being added in increasing quantities to fall-out from the atmosphere of pesticides, fossil fuel wastes, and nuclear wastes from military testing. If these processes continue at their present rate, the best estimate of continuing life is something between fifty and one hundred years. When the oceans die, all other life dies with them.

None of us can surely dispute this fact, yet virtually the entire Lower Mainland uses the Fraser River as a convenient sewer. Victoria does the same with the Strait of Juan de Fuca and we speak of using the atmosphere in the Cariboo as a catchall for tens of thousands of tons of poisonous gas. By a conservative estimate, hundreds of instances of similar abuse abound throughout the province, tens of thousands across Canada, hundreds of thousands throughout the world.

Looking out over an expanse of sunlit ocean, imagining its depth, fluidity and volume, realizing its enormous daily production of life, the idea of destruction, of dead seas rolling murkily upon lifeless shores around the world, is a hard one to grasp. Yet this is exactly the idea, the potential fact, that must be grasped, must be intimately felt and deeply believed by all people everywhere. Survival depends upon it and upon the power of people so informed to control government and industry at all levels – local, national, and international.

24
The Drama of Our Environment
(1970)

My title should really be "The Drama of the Natural Environment." In this context it is important to recognize that dramatic effect exists only in the mind of man. An urban environment is people and of people, controlled or not controlled by people. Its interrelationships are among people, in people and of people and between people; even the stone of its walls and the pavement of its streets is people, the working lives of people, sometimes the working lives of artists and craftsmen. The natural environment has existed for a very long while and quite satisfactorily, entirely without people; it exists now in spite of people; it may be somewhat changed by people, but it will never be controlled by people except here and there, quite temporarily and ineffectively; it will certainly exist again altogether without people. Its dramatic effects are entirely one-sided and unintentional. Perhaps this is its largest dramatic effect.

A dramatic approach to nature, and especially towards animals, has been deliberately used by many modern writers to stimulate interest, affection, and concern for the natural world. Coupled with this concern is a vital dedication to the sharing of transcendental experience, a sense of elation so strong that, even recollected in tranquillity, it cannot be con-

211

tained. Few observers have been more precise than John Henri Fabre. Yet his field was the world of insects – not, one would suppose, intensely dramatic. Open Fabre at any page and the dramatic is there in full form and fashion. The attack pose of the praying mantis: "The wings open to their full size, standing up like parallel screens of transparent gauze, forming a pyramidal prominence that dominates the back. . . . Proudly standing on its four hind-claws, the insect holds its long body almost vertical. The murderous fore-limbs, at first folded and pressed against one another on the thorax, open to their full extent, forming a cross with the body, and exhibiting the axillae ornamented with rows of pearls, and a black spot with a central point of white. These two eyes, faintly recalling those of a peacock's tail, and the fine ebony embossments, are part of the blazonry of conflict, concealed upon ordinary occasions. Their jewels are only assumed when they make themselves terrible and superb for battle." It is all there, observation, interpretation, admiration; descriptions that build dramatic tension and explode into action. Fabre's insects never eat each other, even in the captions to his photographs, they devour each other.

Old-fashioned? Perhaps. Overblown? By some standards. But read it and you cannot in honesty deny its power and dramatic effect. Fabre's writing is a way into a new and unsuspected world. He was a behaviourist and ethologist, rather than an ecologist or an environmentalist. So is Conrad Lorenz.

The animal writers of the late nineteenth and early twentieth centuries owe much, I suspect to Fabre, and achieved much by their debt. Charles Roberts, Seton Thompson, Sir John Fortescue (the librarian of Windsor Castle, not the fifteenth-century jurist), Charles Kingsley, were also behaviourists, depending more strongly than Fabre on anthropomorphic sentimentality for their dramatic effects. Yet it was by dramatic effect that they alerted a large body of readers to the interest and significance of wildlife. With a single short story, Roberts prevented the extinction of the Florida egrets.

None of these writers was fully conscious of environment or of environmental effects, yet they were testing the ground, updating in popular terms the search that led to the greater sophistication of Henry Williamson, Marjorie Rawlings, Fred Bodsworth, and Eric Collier, and eventually to Rachel Carson, George Stewart, and a host of others.

I am aware that I have omitted much of fundamental importance in this brief catalogue – the moods of the English moors and heaths in the Brontes and in Thomas Hardy, the splendours of Herman Melville, the spare dramatics of Hemingway, Dos Passos' love of the land – the list is endless, because no great writer is insensitive to the theme and all of them write with dramatic effect. My purpose is rather to deal with the professed naturalists and to show through them that the natural world has its own unsurpassable dramatic values that inevitably call for expression in dramatic terms.

In my own limited way, I have been a professional in this broad field of writing for nearly forty years, and some personal account of it may not be out of place. I was raised a hunter and a fisherman, and one becomes proficient in these activities only through a sense of ecology. It is the business of both to know where to look. One knows where to look by understanding an animal's response to its surroundings.

I was quite early aware of pollution. I knew that salmon no longer passed upstream of the flax mill below the town (today the mill is closed and I am told they pass that way again). I knew that the trout grew larger below the outlet of the sewage farm. My first battle in the public prints, at the age of sixteen, was over carbolic acid washing into the streams from a coal-tar road dressing. I knew that pheasants were not content with the shelter of coniferous woods, that rabbits could not flourish in wet ground, though many other creatures found their whole being there.

Yet when I left school at seventeen I was not aware that

213

there was such a profession as biology; my understanding was that it was an exercise in the dismemberment of frogs, conducted by unusual types on the modern side. I was not really aware that there had been any attempt to define and systematize the knowledge of the fields and woods and streams.

I intended to write of nature and the natural world as I knew them, and had in fact already written of them before leaving school. My approach, I suppose, was chiefly romantic. Yet I had from the first a very strong opinion, conditioned in some degree by my father's writings, that there was a far better and truer way into the whole subject of wildlife than the anthropormorphic one. Being more writer than naturalist, as I am even today, I was also aware of the difficulty of creating dramatic effects without assigning human or semi-human motivation to wild creatures. Yet I felt that the real power was in fiction, in the making and telling of stories.

At first I settled for factual and descriptive writing, mainly for the outdoor magazines of the time. My first book was a substantial surrender to the anthropormorphic school, the life story of an Atlantic salmon told somewhat in the style of Fortescue's *Story of a Red Deer*. It has remained in print for nearly forty years – in fact the publishers wrote me of a new printing only last week.

My next attempt was to transfer the dramatic burden to something inanimate. I wrote the story of a river and was free then to give an account of all the animals, including man, who lived along it and depended on it. It was a good idea, but I was not really ready for it. In time it seemed naive and derivative, so after two or three editions, I kept it out of print.

In my third book, *Panther,* the dramatic burden is shared between the animals and the hunter. It was a product of painstaking field research, careful observation, much slow-tracking of the animals in the snow, and sceptical distillation of the stories and lore of other woodsmen. I felt it was sound and good. Its dramatic content presumably was sound and good, since it too has remained in print for over thirty-five years and has satisfied a lot of readers.

I am probably oversimplifying, but I think it was at this point that I discovered biology. I was working on what I intended to be a definitive account of the game fish and game fishing of the Pacific Northwest, and doing so as a naturalist and a fisherman, just as I had written *Panther* as a naturalist and a hunter. Then I became aware of the Pacific Biological Station at Nanaimo and the whole world of scientific papers and scientific research that could advance my purpose. It was a pretty late discovery – I think I was twenty-six at the time – but that's what people mean when they say the schools don't teach the kids the things they need to know.

In large measure this discovery transformed me from what I shall call a romantic naturalist into a modern naturalist; from then on I was fairly well aware of whatever knowledge there was and where it could be found. Far from inhibiting dramatic values, I believe this enhances them. Every question accurately answered raises two others still to be answered. Nothing exists by itself, everything is interdependent. The body of a fish, holding place in a stream, is a reflection of the whole watershed and everything else that lives within it.

A writer responds, whatever he may say, to outside pressures, however dimly perceived – pressures of living, of publishers, of the changing outside world; pressures of the desire to communicate (or not to communicate), of the message to be delivered or denied, even the pressures of what he has already written. By taking thought, I daresay I might be able to account for some of the changes in my approach to writing about the natural world, but it really doesn't seem worth while. When I finished *Return to the River,* in 1940, I felt I had gone about as far as I could with the accurate telling of a natural story of a natural animal in its natural world – in other words with animal fiction. I turned more and more to factual and even semi-didactic writing about wildlife and environment. I indulged in some special pleadings (as they seemed at the time, but do not today) and some mild polemics. But I have reserved for myself always the right to emotional considerations and a firmly emotional approach whenever I consider it justified. I do this of necessity. Human emotions exist. They are just as important to humans as other values and sometimes they are just as sound in fact. In recognizing them one has the obligation not to betray truth or destroy truth; one simply acknowledges that some values are less definable and accountable than others.

I will quote a single example. One of my strongest interests and concerns has long been the Pacific salmon runs, not for their commercial value or their value in the sportfishery only, but because of their innate and complex beauty and their symbolic value as the last great abundance of the North American continent. This last in itself is an emotional value, though it involves or should involve something more than that – the self-respect and legitimacy of mankind. If, with the knowledge and understanding we now have, we allow this to be destroyed, we ourselves are nothing very important.

My effort has been to build sympathy and understanding for the salmon. Long ago I realized that many people, seeing the salmon only in their last stages of breeding, felt contemptuous of their "ugliness" and resentful of what seemed to them the waste of their death. There are, of course, quite valid and practical reasons for both phenomena, and I have explained them. But an emotional response is rarely satisfied by practical explanations. So I have explained farther, in writing and in film, that the bodies of the dying salmon are like fallen leaves; that life continues in the fertile eggs under the nursing gravel, as it does through the winter in the roots and sap of dormant trees.

I am not enthusiastic about easy generalizations, but it is probably not too much to say that through most of the world's history the dramatic concerns of the countryman

216

have been primarily with man's place in nature, while urban man has been primarily concerned with man's place in relation to his fellow man. Since dramatic sophistication tends to be urban, and industrial civilization has fostered cities, dramatic emphasis has been on the latter concern. No doubt it will continue to be so. But within the last ten or twelve years, and within the last two or three years especially, urban man has become desperately aware of his environment outside the city walls as well as within them.

I confess I have always resented the city man's contempt for bucolic concerns, as well as his ignorance about the sudden conversion. But there has been suddenness for all of us. If the concerns are not new to the countryman, their immediacy and their comprehensiveness are new. For years we have been fighting long, slow causes against overwhelming opposition. Suddenly those same causes have taken on the immediacy of desperation and we have allies, or seeming allies, on every hand. There can be no question that this has changed dramatic emphasis and quality.

Rachel Carson wrote splendidly dramatic, perhaps overly dramatic, books entitled *The Sea Around Us* and *The Edge of the Sea*. These are environmental books in the best sense. But *Silent Spring* brought the new message to a really wide public, as nothing had before it, precisely because it was dramatic; dramatic in title, in content, and in purpose.

Silent Spring was first published in 1962. Throughout the 1950s ornithologists at several universities had been observing, measuring and reporting the disastrous effects of DDT spraying within their campus areas. They met with surprising resistance and in the face of it even these men of science chose to dramatize their findings by making colour films of dying birds and writing with emotional effect in popular magazines. At least one, whose efforts were suppressed by a university that drew substantial funds from a chemical company, resigned his position.

I mention this because it gives some tiny insight into the forces that have been slowly and painfully developing, ever since World War Two, to produce the present almost universal concern for environmental quality. There have been thousands of small, local dramatizations leading up to the great dramatic realization that environment is life itself; that man's place, if he is to continue to have a place, must be as an integral part of the world environment, not as independent master and shaper.

Now that so many are so suddenly concerned, dramatization of man's dependence on the interdependent nature of his environment takes many forms. Mankind has always taken a somewhat perverse pleasure in predicting its own imminent destruction – the impending Day of Judgment, Day of Wrath, Flood, Fire, or Pestilence. People have believed, and it has not happened; but it seems in the nature of man to know that it must happen eventually. Today it can be rationally forecast in a half-dozen convincing ways. Perhaps the most dramatic statement is that it has already happened, that mankind is simply living out a brief span while the poisons that he has let loose are doing their work. A more purposeful statement is that we still have time to reverse the process, but that time is very short. The Day of Wrath is at hand and it will take some very practical forms of repentance to avert it.

So the Drama of Environment is coming into its own again. Jim Morrison of The Doors sings: "What have they done to the earth? / What have they done to our fair sister?" and renders some soft and brutal answers.

New York's Channel 13 asked ten Off-Broadway playwrights to write on pollution and they all did so. One short sketch, "The Most Beautiful Fish," by Ronald Ribman, had a special appeal for me. It describes a boy and a girl fishing from a wharf in the polluted Hudson River, perhaps now, perhaps a few years from now. Eventually the boy lands a foul, amorphous, gelatinous creature and the girl exclaims in pleasure: "How beautiful salmon are." The boys answers: "How *very* beautiful salmon are." And the playlet ends.

Perhaps the earth sculptors, the plastic sculptors, the minimal sculptors, and the non-sculptors are, as some of them claim, environmentalists. To me they seem more nearly engineers, lagging back in the brief period of technology's ascendancy, insensitive to environment, expressing an arrogant will to overwhelm and conquer it. Christo can package a building and no great harm is done. But when some other believer in "the positive value of large size" packages a beach in plastic, how much life has he killed? The drama of arrogance is not the drama of environment.

The dramatic discovery of the century is that the earth, far from being massive, imponderable, and inexhaustible, is small and finite. Man must make himself small and humble to live within it rather than a ruthless giant to conquer it. Richard Brautigan has written a superb little book called *Trout Fishing in America*. It is a sprightly, irreverent, dead-pan book, humorous and appealing, in some ways reminiscent of Arlo Guthrie's "Alice's Restaurant," carrying an environmental message – or rather a series of them – as straight and square as a gospeller's sermon. It is the sort of book that expresses the heart and reaches to the heart of the people of today and tomorrow.

This brings me back to my original point, that the drama of environment is not really that at all, but the drama of man in relation to his environment. At a pollution seminar in Aspen, Colorado, in 1963, I suggested that there could be little hope for the future unless we could develop a new type of man in place of the aggressive, ruthless, acquisitive individual we had developed, in the effort to open up a continent. I was warned that "you cannot change human nature." So the great dramatic question poses itself again: What is the nature of man in relation to his environment? or, more specifically: Can man make a rational response to his knowledge of the environment? Can he become sensitive, generous, and considerate to his world and the other creatures that share it with him, or is his nature immutably rooted in blood, sex, and darkness?

The unfolding of the answers will make much of the drama of this generation.

Acknowledgments

Of the pieces in this book, "Alan Roderick Haig-Brown"; "If Armageddon's On"; "Place des Cygnes"; "Pollution for Profit"; "Some Approaches to Conservation"; and "Some Thoughts of Paradise," are previously unpublished. "Writer's Notebook: Influences" and "Crying in the Wilderness: Wildlife" were originally CBC broadcasts. "An Outsider Looks at Education"; "The Quality of Living"; and "The Drama of Our Environment" were originally speeches, as were the two Library Association Bulletin pieces.

With the exception of the above, the pieces in this book originally appeared in the following publications:

American Library Association Bulletin
"The Way into Books"

B.C. Outdoors
"Our Ocean: Garbage Dump and Cesspool"

Canadian Library Association Bulletin
"How Important is Reading?"

Canadian Literature
"The Writer in Isolation"

Field and Stream
"Izaak Walton: His Friends and His Rivers"

Maclean's Magazine
"Coastscape"
"Ghost Cat"

The New Yorker
"The Bells"

Saturday Night
"Choice for Canadians"

Tamarack Review
"Hardy's Dorset"

UBC Law Review
"The Lay Mind in the Law"

Weekend
"The Passing of Steam"

Western Living
"Little Girls and Horses"